OPUS ULTIMUM

OPUS ULTIMUM

The Story of the Mozart *Requiem*

Daniel N. Leeson

Algora Publishing
New York

LAN 12-22-08
crcb

ISBN: 0-87586-328-0 (softcover)
ISBN: 0-87586-329-9 (hardcover)
ISBN: 0-87586-330-2 (ebook)

Library of Congress Cataloging-in-Publication Data —

Leeson, Daniel N.
Opus ultimum : the story of the Mozart Requiem / Daniel N.
Leeson.
    p. cm.
    ISBN 0-87586-328-0 (pbk. : alk. paper) — ISBN 0-87586-329-9
(hard cover : alk. paper) — ISBN 0-87586-330-2 (ebook)
    1. Mozart, Wolfgang Amadeus, 1756-1791. Requiem, K. 626, D
minor. I. Title.

    ML410.M9L274 2004
    782.32'38—dc22
                                        2004017624

Front Cover: *Mozart's Grave. Flowers and a monument adorn the grave of composer
Wolfgang Amadeus Mozart (1756-1791) in Vienna, Austria.*
© *Ted Streshinsky/CORBIS*
Date Photographed: ca. 1991

TABLE OF CONTENTS

INTRODUCTION

First, I must express my heartfelt gratitude to Eva Einstein, the only descendant of the late and distinguished Mozart scholar, Alfred Einstein. It was she, as owner of her father's estate, who generously granted permission to use "Opus Ultimum!" as the title of this book. Originally used by her father for a 1937 essay on the Mozart *Requiem*, it identifies this noble composition with a designation unmatched in subtlety and nuance.

This is certainly not the first book devoted entirely to Mozart's last work. That honor belongs to Albert Hahn, a German small-town music director whose 1867 volume was written to try and untangle the confusing and often contradictory elements of the work's published history and circumstances.

This volume is not so much a book as it is the world's longest program note about Mozart's final and unfinished work, the *Requiem*. It is not necessary to state which Mozart *Requiem*. He wrote only one. Other compositions of this form need to be preceded by the composer's name for full identification. There is the Verdi *Requiem*, the Fauré *Requiem*, the Berlioz *Requiem*, the Brahms *Requiem*, and many other superb and moving compositions; but Mozart's is recognized with the simplest identification possible: **The** *Requiem*.

1

A century and a half after Hahn, I continue the never-to-be-completed task of trying to explain and clarify the complicated history of this composition, arguably the most studied and written-about piece of music ever composed. The contemplated audience is broad, especially those who know a little about the subject but would like to know more. Anyone wanting to know or reexamine the details of the obscure history of the Mozart *Requiem*, as well as explore the various threads that make up the fabric of that history, should be able to find here many details that clarify elements of the often contradictory and confusing drama.

The logical first question to be asked is this: if the *Requiem* has been so much written about, how does this telling of the tale differ? The response is that, here, the technique of presentation is somewhat divergent; that is, the story is written in a narrative style like that of a program note, not in the form of a scholarly study. As such, it is obliged to be accurate, but it must also be informative and readable.

While there are several excellent, contemporary books devoted exclusively to the *Requiem* and its history, their purpose is not to be casually read, but studied seriously. Here, there are no footnotes, no extended quotations, no references, bibliographies, charts, diagrams, indices, or Köchel numbers. There is no requirement to have a detailed knowledge of music theory. To avoid a plethora of dates, only those needed to place the material in proper historical perspective are present.

This *Requiem* examination is being told as a story, though nothing in it — either the details of the events or the order of their occurrence — is deliberately fictional or exaggerated. While I may have erred in my analysis with respect to certain new interpretations of the evidence (though I don't think so), nothing has been included purely for purposes of casting the golden glow of drama over events. The story has enough of that without adding more. Even a discussion of Mozart's wife's alleged sexual indiscretions and Süssmayr's sexual orientation are included because, peculiarly, these issues are relevant to the *Requiem*'s history.

The reason for taking the storytelling approach derives from a desire to have the substance of this tale read as a tragic but fascinating story — which it is — and not like a scholarly treatise directed to the specialist (with no disrespect intended to scholarly treatises or specialists). It is hoped that this approach does not trivialize, whitewash, or oversimplify any of the tale's complexities. The fundamental course was to have the reader come away with the idea of having been told a great story in as simple but complete an essence as it is possible to do with a tale as complicated and convoluted as this.

Some style details: (1) the word "requiem" refers to the mass for the dead of the Catholic Church, while *Requiem*, presented without qualification, refers to Mozart's final and incomplete composition, a work commissioned to support and add to the emotional power of the Catholic religious service used to celebrate a mass for the dead. The work was not conceived as a concert decoration and there are some who argue very strongly that, as liturgical music in support of a specific religious service, it should never be performed outside of its intended purpose. However, having been involved in close to 150 performances of the work, I have always found that any concert at which it is performed is ennobled by its presence. (2) The word "autograph" is synonymous with "original manuscript" and is used in this sense; it does not refer to anyone's signature. (3) With very few exceptions, the presentation avoids all non-English words. The only significant exceptions to this are the Latin titles of the fifteen separate sections of the *Requiem*. It will be helpful if the reader becomes familiar with them. These titles — the first word(s) heard in each of the fifteen sections when the composition is performed — will always be given by name. Retaining a sense of which section comes before or after what will make the journey a great deal easier. The sections are:

i. *Requiem aeternam* ([Grant them] Eternal rest)

ii. *Kyrie* (Lord [have mercy])

iii. *Dies irae* (Day of wrath)

iv. *Tuba mirum* (The trumpet [shall sound])

v. *Rex tremendae* (King of tremendous [majesty])

vi. *Recordare* (Remember)

vii.*Confutatis* ([When the wicked have been] confounded)

viii. *Lacrimosa* (Tears)

ix. *Domine Jesu/Quam olim* (Lord Jesus/From the seed [of Abraham])

x. *Hostias/Quam olim* (Sacrifice/From the seed [of Abraham])

xi. *Sanctus/Osanna* (Holy/Hosanna [a word used to express adoration])

xii. *Benedictus/Osanna* (Blessed [is he]/Hosanna)

xiii. *Agnus Dei* (Lamb of God)

xiv. *Lux aeterna* (Eternal light)

xv. *Cum Sanctus Tuis* (With your saints)

The reader does not need to know the details, ritual, order, or vocabulary of a requiem mass to follow the story. For non-Catholic music lovers, the use of terms such as Introit, Sequence, Offertory, Communio, etc., may be unfamiliar and are, therefore, not used.

The romantic imagination is overwhelmingly captured by the essence of the tragedy found in the story of Mozart's composition of the *Requiem*. Evidence of this in the English-speaking world may be found in the many fiction stories published by periodicals during the nineteenth and early twentieth centuries, almost all of which have the same common *Requiem*-related theme: the central character dies with his final and most glorious composition unfinished. Alternatively the work may be finished literally moments before his death. Much of this literature appeared in newspapers, journals, and general periodicals.

Before America's Civil War one such story, entitled *Mozart*, was printed anonymously in an unidentifiable source. A clipping of the story was found in the pages of an old book in Virginia in the mid-1990s; it probably appeared in a Richmond newspaper. (This conclusion was made possible by commercial advertisements, printed on the reverse of the brief story, and which make reference to local merchants of that city. The pre-1862 date of the tale is concluded from mention of "Northern Prices" as found in advertisements from companies in Baltimore, Maryland, a state that remained in the Union during the period of hostilities. It is possible but unprovable that this story was written in response to the first American performance of the *Requiem*, which took place in Philadelphia at the church of St. John the Evangelist in 1834.)

Generally, little effort was made to be historically correct in such *Requiem* fiction. More important to the author was conveying the romantic emotions associated with a genius' final composition coupled with his imminent death.

In Mozart, the central character — unidentified except for the title — is a widower, has a daughter named Emilie, and his *Requiem* melody is sung to a hymn beloved by the character's deceased wife. Despite these elements, all totally foreign to Mozart's real life situation, the essence of the romance of the *Requiem* is found from the first words.

"Mozart"

Author Unknown

> The composer threw himself back on his couch, faint and exhausted. His countenance was pale and emaciated, yet there was fire in his eye and the light of joy on his brow that told of success. His task was finished, and the melody, even to his exquisite sensibility, was perfect. It had occupied him for weeks, and though his form was wasting by disease, yet his spirit seemed to acquire new vigor, and already claim kindred with immortality. Now it was finished; and for the first time for many weeks, he sank into a quiet and refreshing slumber.
>
> A slight noise in the apartment awoke him. Turning to a fair young girl who entered, he said "Emilie, my daughter, come near me — my task is over — the requiem is finished. My requiem," he added, and a sigh

escaped him, as present fame and future glory passed
in vivid succession through his mind. The idea, how
soon he must leave it all, seemed for a moment too
hard to endure.

"Oh! Say not so, my father," said the girl interrupt-
ing him, as tears rushed to her eyes. "You must be better, you look better, for even now your cheek has a
glow upon it; do let me bring you something refresh-
ing, for you have had nothing this morning. I am sure
we will nurse you well again."

"Do not deceive yourself, my love," said he. "This
wasted form can never be restored by human aid; from
heaven's mercy alone can I hope for succor; and it will
be granted, my Emilie, in the moment of my utmost
need; yes, in the hour of death will I claim his help,
who is always ready to aid those who trust him.

"The dying father raised himself on his couch, and
said, "You spoke of refreshment, my daughter; it can
still be afforded to my fainting soul; take these notes,
the last I shall ever pen, and sit down to the instrument. Sing with them, the hymn so beloved by your
mother, and let me once more hear those tones which
have been my delight, my passion, since my earliest
remembrance."

Emilie did as she was desired, and it seemed as if
she sought a relief from her own thoughts; for, after
running over a few chords of the piano, she com-
menced in the sweetest voice, the following lines:

"Spirit! Thy labor is o'er,
Thy term of probation is run,
Thy steps are now bound for the untrodden shore
And the race of immortals begun.

"Spirit! Look not on the strife,
Or the pleasures of earth with regret,
Pause not on the threshold of limitless life,
To mourn for the day that is set.

"Spirit! No fetters can bind,

No wicked have power to molest,
There the weary like thee, and the wretched shall find
A heaven, a mansion of rest.

"Spirit! How bright is the road
For which thou are now on the wing,
Thy *home* it will be with thy Saviour and God,
Their loud hallelujahs to sing."

As she concluded the stanza, she dwelt for a few moments on the low, melancholy notes of the piece, and then waited in silence for the mild voice of her father's praises. He spoke not, and with something like surprise she turned toward him; he was laid back upon the sofa, his face shaded in part with his hand, and his form reposed as if in slumber. Starting with fear, Emilie sprang toward him and seized his hand, but the touch paralyzed her, for she sank senseless by his side. He was gone. With sound of the sweetest melody ever composed by human thought, his soul had winged its flight to regions of eternal bliss.

Similar romanticism may be found in paintings, drawings and engravings of the sad event that has so fascinated the human heart. In a 19th-century painting by Henry Nelson O'Neil (next page), a few sheets of music paper from the *Requiem* manuscript rest on Mozart's lap. The two women behind Mozart portray his wife Constanze and her sister Sophie Weber (later Haibel). The man with the pen seated on Mozart's left and depicted as taking dictation represents Franz Xaver Süssmayr. The three standing men represent Benedikt Schack, a tenor who was *The Magic Flute*'s first Tamino, Franz de Paula Hofer, Mozart's brother-in-law, and Franz Gerle, a bass who was *The Magic Flute*'s first Sarastro. The man seated at the foot of the bed is unidentified but appears to have a musical function since he holds music paper. This highly romantic illustration is one of five known paintings that depict an alleged

The Last Hours of Mozart: oil on canvas by Henry Nelson O'Neil (1817-80), Leeds Museums and Galleries (City Art Gallery) UK

gathering reported on by Schack in 1827 to have taken place at 2 p.m. on December 4, 1791, eleven hours before Mozart's death.

THE VERY BEGINNING

It had been less than half a day since Johannes Chrysostomus Wolfgangus Theophilus Mozart stopped composing and put his quill pen down for the final time of his life, in the last few hours of which he was no longer rational. Because his wife Constanze was in another room and on the verge of emotional collapse, her youngest sister, Sophie Weber, was caring for him. It was clear to her that Mozart was growing progressively weaker as his condition, aggravated by multiple, unnecessary, and counterproductive bloodlettings, continued to deteriorate. He raved and slipped in and out of consciousness. His breath was fetid. His grotesquely swollen body was so sensitive to the touch that he could hardly tolerate the feel of his nightshirt, and his body exuded an odor so foul that it was difficult to stay in the room with him. Many years later, his older son Karl, then seven, would remember standing in a corner of the room, terrified at seeing his father's swollen body, and unable to forget the appalling smell of decay.

As Mozart lay there, only partly conscious, his mouth made "puh-puh-puh" motions, cheeks puffing slightly each time his lips moved. Though no one can be certain, some have interpreted this mouth motion as a dream in which, in some deep level of his subconscious, he was playing the trombone solo from the *Tuba mirum*, an unfinished section of the incomplete work whose 80 surfaces of manuscript lay on his writing desk. Someone had placed them there after Mozart made his last entry, while propped up on pillows in his deathbed only hours earlier.

Finally, at fifty-five minutes into the new day of December 5, 1791, he took a shallow breath, expelled it slowly, and stopped living. Mozart, the man who is thought by some to have been the most supreme musical talent ever to grace the face of the earth, was suddenly no more.

His wife, now widow, Constanze, fell to her knees and begged God to take her, too. Beside herself with grief, she climbed into the bed where her husband's body lay, clung to him, and refused to be separated. Finally, before dawn, she and the two children were taken to the home of a family friend. In the midst of this madness, someone arrived to make a death mask of Mozart's lifeless face. The corpse, covered with a cloth, then remained in his study next to the piano until it was removed for religious rites held on the afternoon of December 6. Following that, the body was taken to St. Marx Cemetery, approximately four miles from Vienna, and, due to the lateness of the arrival, was not buried until the morning of December 7. The precise location of his grave is unknown. His former home, now empty and silent, was sealed until all creditors could be identified.

The House Where Mozart Died
Rauhensteingasse 970

Almost exactly thirteen months later, the composition that he left so incomplete that it was unperformable as written, was played in public for the first time. The work was stated to be entirely new, though completed before the composer's death, with credit of authorship given exclusively to Mozart and no one else.

What we are about to examine are the events that secretly transformed an incomplete set of musical blueprints for what was only a part of a composition into what is universally agreed to be one of humankind's greatest treasures.

A complete understanding of the details surrounding that voyage has eluded generations of dedicated scholars, devoted amateurs, fascinated music lovers, and a few polemical eccentrics for more than two centuries. Significant pieces of that story are still unclear, unknown, and, in far too many cases, unknowable. Strangely, one can argue that some important issues about when things happened and who did what are becoming more obscure. To no small degree, the *Requiem* continues to be looked at through eyes as romantic as those of the author of the fictional story, *Mozart*, found in the prologue of this book.

Speculation about some of the events that might have followed Mozart's death has taken on a patina of truth, despite the fact that some of these stories cannot pass tests of reason. Many hypotheses whose intentions are to clarify crumble into dust when probed by rational analysis.

It seems, therefore, that the best place to begin the story of this fabled work is with a review of the few important details about which there is little disagreement. In principle, the tale of the composition of the Mozart *Requiem* ought to be told in two parts. The first should deal with events that occurred during the last nine months of the composer's life; the second should cover the far more uncertain events that may or may not have taken place following his death. However, because some activities of the first time span influence the events of the second in unpredictable ways, this division is occasionally impossible to maintain.

Since we must start somewhere, let it be on Monday, February 14, 1791, with the macabre details of a grim event. With a recounting of those details, the weaving of the tapestry of the *Requiem* begins.

TWO MEMORIALS FOR A TRAGIC EVENT

The Austrian village of Stuppach lies forty-five miles southwest of Vienna. It is an unlikely place to find the starting point of a mystery whose entire story has eluded the most comprehensive historical and musical investigations of the past two centuries. Nevertheless, it is to that village one must go to begin the story of the Mozart *Requiem*.

There is a very large, three-story house in Stuppach, in fine estate today, though it went through a period of deterioration and decay before an early 1990s restoration returned it to its original splendor. Describing the property as "a house" is an understatement, though it was a residence. Referred to locally as "Stuppach Castle," it was grandiose enough for Pope Pius VI to have stayed there as a guest when he traveled from Rome to Vienna to discuss church-state relations with Austrian Emperor Joseph II. (Joseph, who reigned from 1780 to 1790, was a central character in the movie, *Amadeus*, though undeservedly depicted as a dimwit in that drama.)

The meeting between the two men was as a result of the shock to the Catholic Church caused by Joseph's liberality as Emperor. He closed many of the more than 2,100 convents and monasteries throughout the Austrian empire, relaxed church censorship, tolerated pamphlets critical of the church, abolished the crimes of heresy and apostasy, gave rights to the empire's Jews, and permitted as well as encouraged serious educational reforms.

Stuppach Castle, Winter 2003

Stuppach Castle, 1885

At the time of the events to be discussed, Stuppach Castle was the home of a wealthy twenty-eight-year-old Austrian minor nobleman — a count named Franz Paula Josef Anton von Wallsegg (the name appears in various spellings, such as Walsegg, Wallseg, Wallsseck, etc.) — and his twenty-year-old wife, Maria Anna Theresa Prenner Edlen von Flammberg. The Count's wealth was derived principally from the mining of gypsum and he may have been Austria's most important producer and distributor of that substance, though he had large land and forest holdings, too.

The couple had been married only four years, which means that the wife, born in September 1770, was not yet sixteen when she was wed. Contemporary reports declared her to have been exceptionally beautiful, though no images, not even one of her silhouette, have survived. Their wedding — apparently the result of a genuine love match — required a dispensation by the Catholic Church, possibly due to the bride being a minor at the time. However, it was not

Silhouette of Count Wallsegg

uncommon for women to marry at fifteen or sixteen, though societal rules governing marriages of the nobility may have required a minimum age different from that of other social classes. It does not appear to have been a matter of consanguinity because no genetic intersection between the husband and wife has ever been documented. Perhaps some court intrigue was involved. In any case, the union was brief but happy, though without living issue.

As the wife of a wealthy landowner, the bride had a retinue of servants to make her life easier, including gardeners, cooks, valets, ushers, accountants, clerks, bailiffs, a hunt master, and even a dwarf. Still, disease and infection were great equalizers that erased all class distinctions. They were omnipresent, even in isolated areas such as Stuppach, and being both rich and ennobled was no defense.

Somewhere near the very day when Mozart was celebrating his thirty-fifth (and last) birthday, one of the servants on the Count's estate became ill, and died about two weeks later. Then the Countess became ill, her condition possibly related to the servant's death, though this is by no means sure. Whatever the source of her illness, following a period of high fever and vomiting, she died on Monday, February 14, 1791, of "an acute putrid fever," a description pointing to the possibility of a puerperal sepsis, known during the eighteenth century as "childbed fever." This suggests that the cause of her death might have been an infection of the uterine lining following the delivery of a stillborn infant (or else a miscarriage) brought on by care from an attendant with unclean hands.

On the next day she was embalmed, and, on the following day, was placed in the Wallsegg family crypt in the parish church of Schottwien, only four miles from Stuppach. A mass celebrated by the priest, Matteus Richter, was given in her memory. It was to be the first of Countess Wallsegg's three burials.

One month and eleven days following her interment in Schottwien, she was disinterred and her body was transferred back to Stuppach Castle. There she was entombed in a belowground, brick-lined vault located in meadows adjacent to her former home and above which an elaborate monument was erected. Work on the aboveground memorial, which involved cranes and statuary, continued for an uncertain amount of time following her entombment.

Count Wallsegg would continue to live in Stuppach Castle — unmarried and alone, except for servants — for the rest of his life. The forty-one day hiatus between the Countess' first two burials was made necessary by the movement of materials and workmen from Vienna to Stuppach for the creation of her memorial tomb. There she would lie in repose, theoretically, for all eternity. Wallsegg would visit her elaborate tomb adjacent to Stuppach Castle until his death thirty-six years later.

Schottwien Church: Site of Countess Wallsegg's First and Third Burials

The Count was the last male of his line, though one sister, Countess Maria Karola Magdalena Wallsegg, who married Maria Josef Leopold Leonhard Franz Anton Prokop Vincenz Ignaz Wenzel Count von Sternberg, survived him. (We shall briefly meet Wallsegg's sister at a later stage of this story.) At the time of Count Wallsegg's burial in November 1827, his wife's remains were disinterred a second time and transferred back to the Schottwien parish church, where her remains were placed beside her husband in the Wallsegg family crypt, both in double-case coffins. The site had been used as a burial location for the Wallsegg family since 1720. The crypt was reopened one final time in 1889 during general repairs to the church and finally resealed after the laying of a new floor. Today, two plaques commemorate the couple, one on the outside of the church, and a more informative one inside, next to the sealed entrance of the crypt.

The Countess' third burial was partly due to the fact that French soldiers had vandalized portions of her ornate memorial tomb during the Napoleonic wars. And, it is possible that the Count's beneficiary/sister decided to, or had been requested to, arrange to have the couple lie together forever in death. Eventually, the Countess' tomb and its elaborate memorial statuary would be leveled; all trace of it disappeared towards the middle of the nineteenth century. Today, the field is barren.

But the Count had chosen to honor his wife's memory by commissioning two works of art; the elaborate tomb was only the first. The second was a composition of liturgical music to be used in conjunction with the Catholic ritual of a requiem mass. In theory, at least, that ritual with musical accompaniment was intended for perpetual celebration every February 14, the anniversary of the Countess' passing.

The tomb was commissioned from two Viennese specialists in death architecture, Johann Enrici, designer, and Johann Martin Fischer, sculptor. It was modeled after and is believed to have been similar to the tomb of General Field-Marshall Gideon Ernst Freiherr von Laudon, an important Austrian military hero who had died exactly seven months to the day before Countess Wallsegg. Von Laudon's tomb may have a connection to both Wallsegg and the *Requiem*.

So important was this military hero to Austria, and so publicized was his memorial tomb, that an even more elaborate though miniaturized model bearing little resemblance to the actual tomb was publicly displayed in Vienna for fourteen hours a day beginning in early 1791 and continuing for some time. Each hour, a mechanical organ played funeral music specially composed for the occasion, the selected composer changing from time to time, perhaps weekly. This fact, including the composer's name, was advertised in the *Wiener Zeitung*, Vienna's most important newspaper. One of the two Mozart F minor *Fantasies* for mechanical organ is believed to have been the selected composition during the week of March 26. The publicity and admiration for Von Laudon's tomb and commemorations may have influenced Wallsegg.

Von Laudon's tomb and memorial still exist, surrounded by an iron fence in the Hadersdorf suburb of Vienna (though not in the cemetery of Hadersdorf but on Mauerbachstrasse), and shows what the Countess' memorial is believed to have looked like.

The liturgical music requested by Wallsegg to honor his wife's memory was secretly commissioned from Mozart, the selection possibly motivated by his mechanical organ compositions used during the public display of von Laudon's miniaturized memorial. What Wallsegg requested from Mozart was a composition in a form that the composer never before had occasion to write. Specifically, this was to have been his first work of liturgical music in support of a mass for the dead. It turned out to be his last and, in a peculiar way, it did not turn out to be his first.

Sources disagree on the amount of the fee promised Mozart for the *Requiem*, ranging from approximately 7.5 to 15.5 per cent of the fee paid for the tomb. The most commonly accepted estimate is the low-end figure or 225 gulden for the *Requiem* as contrasted with approximately 3000 gulden for the tomb. That fee was a respectable price, in any case, equal to a quarter of the 900-gulden fee he was

Tomb of Gideon von Laudon,
After Which Countess Wallsegg's Tomb is Believed to Have Been Modelled

paid for writing the opera *Cosi fan tutte*, and a little more than half the amount Mozart would have charged for writing an entire opera for the Austrian Imperial Court.

Exactly when Mozart was offered the commission for the *Requiem* is uncertain. It could have been as late as the summer of 1791; but it might also have been simultaneous with or shortly after the commission for the tomb, which was executed almost immediately after the death of Wallsegg's wife. The agreement was complicated by the Count's wish to be granted exclusive ownership of the *Requiem* following its completion, and Mozart's contractual assurances that the commission would remain a secret.

The issue of when Mozart actually began work on the *Requiem* and what factors prevented it from being completed is interesting history, but not critical to the story. He was certainly busy with other things. That included two operas — his fairytale, *The Magic Flute*, and *The Clemency of Titus*, required for the coronation of a new Austrian emperor, following the death of Joseph II. There was also the composition of what would be his final concerto, the one for clarinet.

Exactly when Mozart composed the *Requiem* is unclear and remains controversial. One view holds that it was written over three distinct periods, the first beginning in June or July 1791, and the second in mid-September of that same year. Mozart began the third and final phase around November 15, supposedly ending it only eleven hours before his death.

Fifty-two days before his thirty-sixth birthday, Mozart died in Vienna of causes that remain uncertain to this day. His youthful death was not an uncommon phenomenon in that era. In 1791, the average Viennese life expectancy was less than fifty. Every single person in his parish who died in December 1791, the month of his death, was under the age of fifty-six.

At present, more than 150 different explanations have been offered for his death. These include murder (for profit or from jealousy), accidental suicide (ingestion of mercury taken to cure a venereal disease), political assassination (with accusations of Masonic involvement), accident (fractured skull caused by a fall from a horse), natural causes (heart failure and death by overwork and lack of exercise), medical errors (misdiagnosis along with excessive venesection, or blood letting), and a grotesque array of proposed diseases and illnesses, including but not limited to, apoplexy, Brights disease, chronic nephritis, cirrhosis, deposit on the brain, dropsy, encephalitis, epilepsy, gastritis, goiter, grippe, heated miliary fever, inflammatory fever, meningitis, pneumonia, renal failure, rheumatic fever, Schonlein-Henoch syndrome, streptococcal infection, trichinosis, tuberculosis, typhoid fever, typhus, uremia, and water on the chest.

At the moment of Mozart's death, the 80 surfaces of *Requiem* manuscript paper contained only one short section of 48 measures — approximately 300 seconds of music — that was complete and playable as written (though even this statement must be qualified because some portions of the trumpet and drum music may not be in

Mozart's hand). Sequentially, it was the first in the manuscript, and is referred to as the *Requiem aeternam*.

> Eternal rest grant them, O Lord, and may perpetual light shine upon them. A song of praise in Zion is made to You, O God, and to You the vow shall be performed in Jerusalem. Hear my prayer; to You all flesh shall come. Grant them eternal rest, O Lord, and may perpetual light shine upon them.

In light of the fact that so much of the *Requiem* is incomplete, the use of the word "complete" when speaking about the *Requiem aeternam* requires an explanation. It means that, using only Mozart's manuscript score as a source, extracting individual performance parts for the instrumentalists and singers will permit the reading of a musically complete version of Mozart's conception. The forty-eight manuscript measures that constitute the entire *Requiem aeternam* occupy nine surfaces of paper, plus one measure of a tenth, of the full set of 80 surfaces.

Following the final measure of the *Requiem aeternam*, every one of the rest of the surfaces — excluding the approximately six blank ones that exist between sections — has music written on it, for a total of nine additional sections. However, all those sections are incomplete — a term that requires a much more detailed description to convey the three distinct dimensions of the *Requiem*'s shortcomings. That portion of the manuscript, because of its imperfection, is, as it stands, publicly unperformable.

In effect, except for approximately five minutes of music, the *Requiem* as it existed at the moment of Mozart's death was so incomplete that it could never be heard as a finished composition.

However ...

THE PIVOTAL CHARACTER

Every mystery has a critical central character, one whose behavior engineers the events of the drama. With the *Requiem*, Mozart's wife assumes that role. In opposition to the general perception of the mild, gentle, good-natured *hausfrau* of an eighteenth-century Austrian wife, who kept to the background, cooked the meals, and bore the children, following Mozart's death his widow transformed herself into a master puppeteer. She took control of the situation, managed the details, and, as it suited her purpose, spawned many deliberately false, unclear, and contradictory particulars about the *Requiem*'s creation. Paradoxically, and to her eternal credit, her actions prevented a cultural catastrophe when, by her fierce determination alone, she saved the *Requiem* from loss and destruction, perhaps the world knowing nothing of its existence.

Mozart met his future wife, Maria Constanze Cecelia Josepha Johanna Aloysia Weber, when she was sixteen. He was twenty-one, and in love with her older sister, Maria Aloisia Louisa Antonia Weber (later Lange), a romance that was doomed to failure. Constanze used that name because she, her mother, and two of three sisters all bore the baptismal first name of "Maria." It is thought that at least fifty percent of all women in Austria carried that name, a practice not uncommon in Catholic countries. Sometimes even men bore that name, Constanze's first cousin, composer Carl Maria von Weber, being one example and author Erich Maria Remarque being another.

Mozart's attraction for Constanze began in 1781 and led to their marriage in 1782. His future mother-in-law, who knew very well how to steer an unsophisticated young man into a marriage, finessed the union. Constanze was no beauty, but she loved her husband and bore him six children, of whom only two survived. Following Mozart's death, rumors may have arisen about her alleged promiscuity during her husband's lifetime. Only because these allegations involve the man who completed the *Requiem* — and

Constanze Mozart: Painting Done in 1782 At the Time of Her Marriage

therefore play a role in the work's history — do these assertions have any part in the story.

Hers was a remarkable personality transformation. First, she was a shy young girl who became a loving bride. Next, she was a six-time mother, pregnant for a little more than half her married life (fifty-four out of 102 months), and who may also have had some miscarriages, too. With respect to her role in the *Requiem*'s completion, she appears to have metamorphosed into a scheming, unscrupulous, selfish, and dishonest woman who holds primary responsibility for much of the confusion and misinformation about the composition's evolution.

In order for Constanze to satisfy the terms of the agreement between her late husband and Count Wallsegg, she initiated a series of activities to have a performable version of the *Requiem* created.

The completed work was to be based on the musical torso left at her husband's death. It would then be delivered, falsely identified as entirely Mozart's conception and execution, to Count Wallsegg's agent. To this end, Constanze solicited the assistance of some uncertain number of people, the last of whom, Franz Xaver Süssmayr, provided what she needed.

The completed *Requiem* was delivered to Count Wallsegg's agent in satisfaction of the original commission sometime in the first half of 1792 — the exact date is uncertain. *What this thing was that Count Wallsegg received, who accomplished what to create it, and the various other matters that constitute the tale of its production, are the heart of the Requiem story.*

In effect, most of the important details about what happened prior to Mozart's death are known or can be accounted for by reasonable speculation. But almost everything that happened following his death is cloaked in a haze of mystery, speculation, wishful thinking, and dishonesty, and can only be understood with a great deal of informed guesswork. Humankind's nature at its very best can be found in the story. At its worst, too.

TAKING CONTROL

Immediately after Mozart's death — perhaps as little as eight days later — Constanze began to supervise the events that would eventually get the *Requiem* completed and delivered to Wallsegg's agent. Considering the fact that she was not even supposed to know about the secret commission, why was she motivated — even compelled — to undertake this effort so quickly? Two possible explanations may clarify her behavior.

The first and most obvious is that a completed *Requiem* would bring in some badly needed money. Clearly, she knew something about the commission despite the confidentiality agreement imposed on Mozart. There is even some evidence that Mozart (and, therefore, Constanze) might have known the name of the man who had commissioned the work. It is also possible that she knew how much was still pending, namely the balance due upon completion. It is less likely that Mozart told her how much he had already been paid — that was money of the past, and Mozart's financial situation had been much more attuned to money of the now and of the future.

The second possibility lending haste to her quest for a completed *Requiem* involves a hypothetical inquiry from Wallsegg's agent. While the least modicum of respect and tact would prevent them from pressing too immediately upon the recently bereaved with a business matter, Constanze might have received some kind of communication from Wallsegg's agent — a question about the status of the commission — within a few days of her husband's death. What form this contact might have taken — if it took place at all — is unknown. It could have been a visit, or a written communication, perhaps. Its purpose would have been to advise Constanze that her husband had accepted a commission to compose a *Requiem* — this, theoretically, being news to her — that the agent was acting as intermediary for an anonymous commissioner, that certain sums had been paid in advance, and that the balance due would be paid immediately upon delivery of the composition.

1840 Daguerreotype Of Constanze Mozart in Altötting,
Bavaria at the 70th Anniversary Celebration of a
Friend, Max Keller

The agent would have apologized for bringing this matter up at such an inopportune time, noting by way of excuse that the unnamed commissioner had already laid out a great deal of money and, on hearing of Mozart's death, expressed concern. Would the widow please be so kind as to let the agent know whether, and when, he might receive the composition that he had contracted from her late husband and on which a partial payment had been made?

Constanze was no fool and would have read between the lines of the request. Not only was there a prize to be won by producing a completed work, but a veiled threat was there, as well. Failure to present a completed *Requiem* would almost certainly have obliged her to repay all sums advanced to her late husband. This was money she did not have.

Thus, whether on her own or upon being prodded by the agent of the *Requiem*'s commissioner, Constanze recognized the necessity to act, and at once.

While the above reward/punishment-avoidance scenario is entirely invented, her behavior within approximately a week of her husband's funeral indicates that something of this nature must have taken place. This is because, as we shall see very shortly, on or about December 13, the eighth day of her widowhood — and possibly earlier — she took her first steps to get someone to complete the *Requiem*.

1856 Daguerreotype Of Mozart's Son Karl In
Salzburg During The Centennial Commemorating
His Father's Birth

Meanwhile, if the invented scenario about a communication from Wallsegg's agent really did happen, she would have been obliged to respond to the inquiry. It would not have been a difficult letter to write. She could maintain that she was not aware of any such commission, but she would certainly look through her late husband's many compositions for one of the nature described. Right now, however, things were in a terrible mess and her husband's estate was in disarray. As soon as she had some information, she would be sure to inform the agent of what she found.

Constanze would have known intuitively that any effort to have someone complete the *Requiem* would require absolute secrecy. She must have recognized that to present what would be partially a forgery as a work composed entirely by her late husband would be grounds for ruinous legal action. However, even before Mozart died, a small cadre of people was aware of his efforts on a composition of a religious nature — a composition that he might not be able to complete. For example, with his involvement, portions of the *Requiem* were said to have been sung at his deathbed only hours before he died. But this was a small group and it could be controlled.

Realistically, Constanze had three choices. She could have sent the unfinished score — and she knew exactly where it was — to Wallsegg's agent and tried to get away with it. Had she taken that action, it is almost certain that the work would have been lost to the world forever. As will be shown at a later stage of this story, this is by no means a melodramatic exaggeration. Such a horrific conclusion would almost certainly have occurred, even had Mozart himself completed the composition and personally delivered it to Wallsegg's agent prior to his death. When we examine the actions and character of Count Wallsegg — as well as the disposition of his estate following his death — we shall see that it was the paradox of the *Requiem* being incomplete, coupled with Constanze's efforts to get it completed, that probably enabled its survival.

Constanze's second choice — to do nothing — was not a practical alternative. Eventually, Wallsegg would have demanded his deposit back. Furthermore, though no such document has ever been found, Wallsegg almost certainly had a formal contract for delivery of the *Requiem* and Constanze would have known it. He was a businessman and would not have been such a fool as to disperse money for ordered merchandise without a formal agreement. In effect, he had unshakable grounds for getting his money back if Constanze claimed to know nothing about the matter.

Fortunately for Constanze — and this was something about which she could not have known at this juncture — there seems to have been an as yet unexplored dimension of the *Requiem*'s commission, one that had the explosive potential of publicly humiliating Wallsegg. Specifically, if it became public knowledge that the hypothetical contract of commission included clauses about confidentiality and surrendering of author ownership, such peculiar demands would have raised questions and cast light into a corner of Wallsegg's life that he wanted very much to keep private. Later, in a brilliant but ruthless way, Constanze would use Wallsegg's desire to remain behind the scenes on this matter as a tactical weapon against him.

However, a contract is a contract, and Wallsegg would have won his case, had it come to that. These conclusions would have been obvious to Constanze, and she saw that taking no action at all simply would not do.

Her third choice — to get the composition completed — was risky, but it was the only remotely acceptable alternative among unpalatable options. And because she did what she did, the world owes a debt of infinite gratitude to her. Had she acted in almost any other way, the consequences become too terrible to contemplate. Whatever her motivation, her efforts rescued one of the world's most sublime masterpieces from oblivion and almost certain destruction.

However, praise for her effort cannot be given without simultaneously reporting that her subsequent behavior to achieve her ends was, as we shall see, unethical in many specifics. To protect herself, she frequently resorted to outright falsification of facts. This has resulted in casting doubt on many of her utterances about the details of the *Requiem*'s history. Unfortunately, it goes well beyond that. Because of her behavior with respect to the completion of the *Requiem*, almost everything she said about Mozart, his life, and his music is tainted and must be viewed with considerable skepticism.

Constanze had little money and a great deal of debt. Her husband had died a pauper; her financial situation was desperate, and she had two young sons to raise: Karl, seven, and Franz Xaver, an infant only four months old. Except for her friends and family, who could provide only limited financial assistance, she was essentially alone in the world.

Mozart's widow was not a well-trained musician. She is said to have had a pretty voice; she played the piano, could sing nicely, and read music, but it is uncertain that she fully understood the extent of her husband's gifts at this juncture of her life. Indeed, few people then alive could understand the awesome power of his musical intellect. It is unlikely that she could read a full score, identify the details and purpose of any of her husband's sketches, or even conclude to what composition a particular unidentified sketch might apply. Her belief appears to have been that Mozart's greatness lay in his ability to create melody. To her musically unsophisticated mind, given a Mozart tune, someone of lesser talent might produce results equivalent to his by using his sketches as high-quality raw material for an entire composition.

Either she or someone close to her with more sophisticated musical skill must have examined the manuscript of the *Requiem* almost immediately after Mozart's death. If she did the examination, then her lack of serious musical training would probably have caused her erroneously to conclude that the work required only modest effort to complete it. If someone with experience did the examination, that person might have suggested caution, considering the unfinished state of the composition. Whichever the case, from her musically unsophisticated point of view, the work was practically finished — causing her to throw caution to the winds and take the position that one of her late husband's musical acquaintances could complete it quickly, a note here, a note there.

It can be argued persuasively that, initially at least, she might not have realized that her actions could be perceived as being deceptive. She saw the composition as virtually complete. The idea that the work, as it then existed, was too short for liturgical use would have been beyond her musical capacity, since the matter of what constituted a satisfactory musical accompaniment to a requiem mass was (and is) a complicated subject. What she saw were 80 surfaces of manuscript with music on them, all in her husband's hand. And if a passage here or there was not fully developed, she believed that fixing things up would not affect the overall authorship, the essential character, or the basic nature of the work. It may well be that some of the things that would later be seen as having been duplicitous were, in her eyes, not intended as such.

Her realization that she could reverse her immediate financial woes drove her to have the work completed. This, in turn, influenced all of the activities that followed, not only over the next few months but to a considerable degree for the rest of her life.

She would be buried in 1842, and her two children in 1844 (Franz Xaver) and 1858 (Karl). All three would be laid to rest with the now-completed music of the *Requiem* played and sung for them in memoriam by an orchestra, chorus, and vocal soloists.

This, then, describes the state of affairs as she went into action almost immediately after her husband's passing. During the period of approximately eight days, between his death and her first attempts to have the work completed, the shy, quiet, and retiring Constanze metamorphosed into an iron-willed, determined, and ruthless woman.

SELECTING THE COMPLETER

The first person who agreed to undertake the completion of the *Requiem* appears to have been the Viennese musician Joseph Leopold von Eybler, though Constanze may have invited others (about whom we have no knowledge) before him. The earliest evidence that she was actively pursuing such an effort derives from a document dated December 21, just sixteen days after Mozart's death. In it, Eybler agrees to make the completion, stating only what his commitments would be, not what Constanze might provide in return. He obligates himself to complete the *Requiem* "by the middle of the coming Lent, and ... guarantee[s] that it shall neither be copied nor given into hands other than those of the ... widow," meaning Constanze, of course.

Exactly what understandings were reached privately between

The Mozart children in 1798

the two of them, financial or otherwise, are unknown. Since she had little to offer in any case, it is presumed that he agreed to do the work without fee, entirely out of respect for Mozart. On the other hand, as we shall see, he eventually became owner of a portion of the original *Requiem* manuscript. What he had was of such stupendous

Eybler estimated at around 30 years of age

financial value that it would be difficult to establish its worth today, though several million dollars is not an outrageous figure.

Eybler's musical competence had strong supporters, including Beethoven's teacher, Johann Georg Albrechtsberger, who said that, except for Mozart, Eybler was the greatest musical genius in all of Vienna. Even Mozart had written a testimonial praising his knowledge of composition.

Though Eybler appears to have begun quickly, he soon abandoned the effort; but not before writing many of his ideas directly on Mozart's original manuscript. That was an unfortunate decision. His additions left the autograph in such a state that whoever was to undertake the task after him would be required to construct an entirely new score. Not only did Eybler not complete the work, he complicated the task for any person coming after him, who would have to deal not only with Mozart's manuscript, but also with Eybler's additions to it.

No reason is known why Eybler refused to finish the task, abandoning it after completing only five sections and beginning a

Eybler estimated at 70 following his having had a stroke

sixth (from the *Dies irae* up to the *Lacrimosa*, where he stopped work after adding two measures to the choral soprano line). The fact that he withdrew from the work at that point is revealing. The *Lacrimosa* is the most incomplete of all the sections begun by Mozart, and this may have represented a task that he felt was beyond him. Alternatively, it is possible that he realized his inability to conclude the work by "the middle of the coming Lent," and withdrew for that reason. Another and more simple motivation behind his withdrawal could be related to the fact that it was too much for him to do without getting paid.

With the abandonment of his agreement, Eybler leaves the story of how the *Requiem* was completed, though not his involvement in its history. For one thing, as mentioned earlier, he became owner of part of the manuscript, though how and when he got hold of it is uncertain. Prior to his death, he donated that material to what is today Vienna's Austrian National Library. Eighteen years after he voided his agreement to finish the work, he conducted it (presumably in the completion of his successor, Franz Xaver Süssmayr) at a Viennese memorial service for Franz Joseph Haydn. Finally, in Vienna on February 23, 1833, he suffered a stroke while conducting the work, though he lived, partially paralyzed, until 1846 when he died at the age of 80-one.

It is possible that, upon being informed of Eybler's withdrawal, Constanze asked a number of people to take on the task before she found someone willing to do it. If that is the case, such invitations are not documented. Eventually, Franz Xaver Süssmayr, about whom a great deal needs to be said, was invited to undertake the completion. He agreed, did the job, and the rest, as they say, is history, though it is history in its most complicated, tangled, and bewildering form.

SÜSSMAYR, AND CONSTANZE'S CONSTANCY

In some of the *Requiem* literature, Süssmayr is said to have been Mozart's pupil. But there is a problem with that statement. The source for the assertion is implied in letters written by Constanze Mozart, one of which, dating from 1826, explicitly used the word, "pupil" to describe the relationship. However, her assertions about *Requiem* circumstances are frequently unreliable and no hard evidence exists elsewhere to supports that view.

Mozart and Süssmayr appear not to have known each other prior to 1790, though that would certainly have been enough time for Süssmayr to have learned something, if actual study had taken place. Two fifty-year-old scholarly studies contradict each other about Süssmayr's status as a Mozart pupil. One study, listing sixteen composition students and twenty-two piano pupils during Mozart's lifetime, states without giving independent evidence that

Süssmayr was a composition student. The other study divides the list of Mozart's pupil-candidates into three categories: those who were certain to have studied with him, those who probably were his students, and those who were not his pupils. Süssmayr is found in none of the categories.

It is suggested here that no evidence supports the assertion that Mozart gave Süssmayr any formal compositional instruction. In fact, judging from the technical aspects of his work on the *Requiem*, it appears that Süssmayr's musical training was not thorough. However, it would have been impossible for the younger man to work with such a master, as he allegedly did in the production of the opera, *The Clemency of Titus* (an assertion that is also fraught with difficulties), and learn nothing. But the idea of Süssmayr having had a formal student relationship to Mozart is one of the many stories about the *Requiem* that cannot be confirmed.

Constanze's assertion of a teacher/pupil relationship may have arisen because she wished to give the impression that lessons from Mozart would have enabled Süssmayr to compose like her husband. Such an oversimplified view might be expected from someone with only an amateur's understanding of the technical issues involved. By asserting that Süssmayr had been her husband's pupil, Mozart's creative influence on the end product would be increased and Süssmayr's work would be relegated to that of a clerk. Thus, the teacher/pupil stratagem could have been invented to suggest, naively, that Süssmayr was a vessel through which Mozart's skill and talent would pass unchanged; that is, Süssmayr would produce nothing that Mozart would not have produced.

However, this story of an alleged pupil-teacher relationship is not the most important of the several mysteries that surround the Mozart/Süssmayr connection. Another, more important to the *Requiem*'s history, involves the relationship between Süssmayr and Constanze.

The history of Süssmayr's involvement with the *Requiem* is a festival of anomalies, with one of them being the source of distasteful stories about Constanze Mozart's alleged sexual indiscretions. Under normal circumstances, a discussion of this subject would have little or nothing to do with a particular composition's history. However, the selection of Süssmayr — or, more accurately, the matter of the initial non-selection of Süssmayr — has become a breeding ground for claims that amount to character assassination.

As previously mentioned, Constanze had first invited Joseph Eybler to complete the *Requiem* and, on December 21, 1791, he agreed to do so. Assuming that her request and his agreement were not simultaneous, she probably first broached the subject with him a few days earlier, perhaps a week. This would place her request, the theoretical first step in the sequence of events aimed at getting the *Requiem* completed, on or around December 15, the tenth day after Mozart's death.

Eybler began work, not, as one might think, with the second section of the *Requiem*, the *Kyrie*, but with the third, the Dies Irae. This is because the *Kyrie* had already been made complete in preparation for a memorial service held for Mozart on December 10. On that date, the first two sections of the *Requiem* — the *Requiem aeternam*, composed entirely or almost so by Mozart, and the *Kyrie*, drafted by Mozart but completed on or before December 10 by an uncertain number of people, one of whom was Süssmayr — are said to have been performed in Vienna's Church of St. Michael.

After Eybler reneged and withdrew from the task of completing the *Requiem*, there follows a period of uncertain duration during which it is said that Constanze was unsuccessful in getting someone else to complete the work, though whom she might have asked is unknown. Finally, she approached Süssmayr who accepted the task and did the job.

That appears to be a straightforward story with no obvious complications. Why should this chain of circumstances be spoken of as anomalous?

Whenever a sequence of events occurs in an order that doesn't appear to make sense, one is forced to ask why things happened that way. And in this case, the described sequence does not seem rational. Süssmayr should have been asked first. He was the logical candidate. Supposedly, he and Mozart had conversations about how to complete the work. Further, he had experience in making a completion by virtue of his participation in the efforts to make the *Kyrie* performable, an event believed to have been done in the five days between Mozart's death on December 5 and the memorial service on December 10.

Fully thirty-six years later, in a letter to a family friend, Constanze commented on this very issue, saying "My asking Eybler to finish it came about because I was annoyed with Süssmayr at the time (I don't remember why)..." This response added further fuel to already existing rumors about a sexual relationship between the two.

These rumors include, but are not limited to, the following assertions. First, that her last child, Franz Xaver Wolfgang Mozart, born a little over four months before her husband's death, was actually fathered by Süssmayr; and, as evidence to support the assertion, the child bears Süssmayr's first two names.

Second, that she wanted Süssmayr to marry her, and that she might have proposed this to him and been rejected was really the source of her anger.

Third, that Mozart knew of the affair — alluding to the possibility of a ménage à trois — since the child's name seems to signify that Mozart was aware of who the real father was.

And, fourth, that by acknowledging and tolerating Süssmayr as Constanze's escort while both were in Baden — she for treatment of varicose veins, Süssmayr for uncertain reasons — he had encouraged the relationship.

So a simple question about a sequence of events — why not Süssmayr first? — has further burdened the history of the *Requiem* with unsavory accusations about how Constanze might have violated her marriage vows.

The accusation about the paternity of Franz Xaver Wolfgang Mozart would be dealt with at a later time, though in a fashion that ultimately has proven to be clumsily transparent. It had to do with the child's deformed left ear. A biography of Mozart compiled by Constanze's second husband, Georg Nikolaus Nissen, contains a drawing of the son's ear falsely advertised as Mozart's ear. This may have been an attempt to demonstrate that the deformity, presumably inherited — but, in fact, derived from intrauterine pressure — appeared in both, a tactic possibly designed to blunt accusations of infidelity.

I suggest that the evidence points to the possibility that these fanciful and unflattering stories — quite irrelevant to the history of the *Requiem* of which they have become a part — are totally false. And the reason for this conclusion derives from observations about Süssmayr's lifestyle. I suggest that he was exclusively homosexual, and that it is unlikely that he ever had a sexual relationship with any woman, including Constanze.

While this assertion has no smoking gun to confirm it — any more than with the theory of Constanze's alleged affair with Süssmayr — the pieces are all there and they fit together. There are bits of evidence about Süssmayr's life that tend to lead in this direction, and while that does not mean it is true, the evidence supporting the accusations of his alleged affair with Constanze is far less substantial than the evidence suggesting his possible homosexuality. So, what is the evidence?

On July 2, 1791, Mozart wrote a letter to his wife, then pregnant and staying in Baden while undertaking treatment for varicose veins. In the letter, three very curious and possibly revealing items appear. In a comment about Süssmayr — whom he knew was also in Baden at that moment, though he did not necessarily know the reasons for him being there — Mozart suggested, in a literary backslapping fashion, that Constanze give "a thousand boxes on the ear for Lacci Bacci." What do these words mean?

Mozart liked to give rhyming, silly-sounding names to people, including himself. A letter of his, from early 1787, lists "Hinkiti Honky," "Punkitititi," "Schabla Pumfa," "Rozka Pumpa," "Natschibinitschibi," "Sagadarata," "Runzifunzi," "Schurimuri", and

"Gaulimauli," among others. In that context, the words "Lacci Bacci" might mean nothing.

However, as Hungarian homonyms, those words are not necessarily nonsense syllables but can be perceived as misspellings of "Laci bácsi" (pronounced "LAT-see BAT-chee"), which translates to "Uncle Laci," this being an affectionate nickname for "Uncle Laszlo." At the time of Mozart's use of "Lacci Bacci," Hungary was part of the Austrian empire and some Hungarian phrases crept into the Viennese idiom.

Manuscript material located in the two most important libraries in Budapest show that the words "laci" and "bácsi" were found to have had a suggestive, indecent, and scandalous history of sexual meanings throughout the recorded period of Hungarian slang.

The word "bácsi," for example, forms part of the Hungarian expression, "kosaras bácsi," or "man with a basket," which was used to describe old men who attracted young boys and girls with presents contained in their baskets. An example from 1908 states, "In the city park ... during spring and summer, walk the men with baskets looking for victims."

The two words "kosaras bácsi" appear in another slang dictionary as a single word, "kosarasbácsi," explicitly defined as a homosexual. Further, it is stated to be synonymous with another word, also containing the root "bácsi," and which translates to "man with a bouquet."

As for "Laci," several words that use it as a root ("Lacisik" and "Lacizni," for example) are obscene synonyms for intercourse. Here, a name, "Laci," has been transformed into the verbs "Lacisik" and "Lacizni." It is a manner of speech for which it is difficult to find a parallel in English, although "Jack" can convey roughly the same sense.

What all of this says is that, at uncertain times in Hungarian vulgar speech, variants of the words "Laci" and "bácsi", independently or in conjunction with other words, took on sexual meanings that explicitly included homosexuality. Today, native

Hungarian speakers have no knowledge of this meaning of the term "Laci bácsi"; but that is a not-uncommon phenomenon in the use of code words and slang, whose meanings change, grow cold, or disappear with time.

So the cryptic words "Lacci Bacci," as used by Mozart in his letter to his wife, are not necessarily nonsense syllables. They have meaning, invariably sexual, often scandalous (though not in German).

The same Mozart letter to his wife contains two other peculiar things, both of which can be interpreted to point to the same conclusion; that is, that Süssmayr was a homosexual. In the letter, he writes: "I have just had a visit from a couple of Englishmen... But of course the real truth is that they wanted to meet that great fellow Süssmayr and only came to see me in order to find out where he lived... They want to engage him to clean the lamps." While Mozart may have meant that the two visitors were from England, another possibility has to be considered.

Homosexuality was at various times referred to as "The English Disease," a term with a long history of use as a coded expression for something else, and made at the expense of the English. At various times, it was used for rickets (a disease caused by a vitamin D deficiency), a national predisposition for strikes and social unrest, the upper class' penchant for political and sexual scandals (as in the Profumo affair of the 1960s), and, most recently, for soccer hooliganism.

A not uncommon practice was to associate nationality with a particular disease, often sexually transmitted. For example, the English called syphilis "The French Disease"; the French called it "The Italian Disease"; the Italians called it "The Turkish Disease"; the Russians called it "The Polish Disease"; and both the Japanese and the Indians termed it "The Portuguese Disease." Only the Spanish accepted any blame, referring to it as "The Spanish Disease."

In this context, the otherwise incomprehensible reference in Mozart's letter to "cleaning lamps" can be interpreted as a request for a specific sexual act.

Add to this the fact that Süssmayr never married, and that there are no confirmable cases of his having had a romantic attachment with any woman. This hypothesis would appear to be weakened by a letter Süssmayr wrote to a friend shortly before his death on September 17, 1803, in which Süssmayr spoke of his intentions to marry. But this objective, even if it was real, does not disprove his possible homosexuality. Social pressure has often led homosexual men to marry and even to father children to disguise or deny their sexual preference. Oscar Wilde, Leonard Bernstein, and Rock Hudson may have been such cases.

A second Mozart letter, written to his wife one week before the "Lacci Bacci" letter quoted above, provides additional insight into what may have been Mozart's knowledge of Süssmayr's sexual orientation. On June 25, 1791 Mozart wrote, "I advise you not to go to Mass tomorrow. Those peasant louts are too cheeky for my taste. True, you have a rough companion but the peasants don't respect him ... as they see at once that he is 'a silly ass.'"

None of the traditional scholarly texts devoted to the study of Mozart's correspondence has ever been able to translate the German word "schaberl," given above in a translation by Emily Anderson as "a silly ass" and, apparently, used by Mozart only once in the entire collection of his extant letters. Other attempts to find the meaning of this still-unknown German word have suggested that perhaps Mozart meant "shabby" or propose that Süssmayr was "a bit of a miser." But in context, it is difficult to accept any of these interpretations. An important question is why would Süssmayr not be respected? One possibility is that Mozart employed a now-unknown (or entirely invented) word that was intended to be the equivalent of a rough and ugly condemnatory phrase formerly used to refer to a homosexual man, namely "a queer," though this is impossible to confirm.

The author put the question to the man who is considered by some to be the world's leading authority on scandalous early German expressions, Professor Sander Gilman, Chair of the Department of Germanic Studies at the University of Chicago. He confirmed that he could find no reference to "schaberl" or any variation of it in standard dialect compilations. He concluded that it was either a private term or else one that was so scabrous that it was deliberately not recorded by the prudish compilers of the various Austrian dialectic dictionaries and lists. His sense of the word in the context of the passage in Mozart's letter was that Süssmayr was considered "schaebig" (from High German), with the implications of being "scabrous." By the late seventeenth century, the word had come to mean diseased and ugly, a term with the moral overtones towards homosexuality and other forms of sexual pathology, such as syphilis. Professor Gilman's conclusion was that "schaberl" as used by Mozart is a scabrous word that means "scabrous."

Beginning at age fourteen, Süssmayr had a lifelong personal friendship with Pater Georg Pasterwitz, a priest whom he would occasionally meet in Baden. According to an unconfirmed report personally communicated to the author — and which considerable effort, time, and expense has been unable to confirm — Baden police records are said to state that the two used the same hotel, "Die Kröne" — though there is no mention that they shared the same room — at the time Mozart tolerated his wife being escorted by Süssmayr. Baden was then a city that was a haven for dandies on the prowl, which could well have been Mozart's primary concern for Constanze, as well as a notorious homosexual hangout, both allegations confirmed by tour guides of the area even today.

As a young student, Süssmayr went to Kremsmünster Abbey, where he became the favorite pupil of Pasterwitz, the school's music teacher. When Pasterwitz was transferred to Vienna, Süssmayr followed him to that city, which is how he began work in the Viennese milieu, performing a variety of tasks including acting as a music copyist for Mozart's supposed nemesis, Antonio Salieri. The possibility of a sexual relationship between a priest and a young boy — one that lasted into the younger man's adulthood — was not impossible then any more than it is now. Süssmayr's death followed that of Pasterwitz by only a few months.

As for Mozart's tolerance of Süssmayr escorting Constanze in Baden, it could not have a simpler solution. Mozart had two concerns: to protect Constanze from the dandies of that city, and to choose a man whose intentions he need not doubt. I suggest that the dandies in Baden were much more dangerous to the security of Constanze's marriage vows, to say nothing of her purse, than Süssmayr ever was. The fact that she was no beauty, eight months pregnant, and had troublesome varicose veins would not have deferred the pursuit of a determined roué in the slightest.

I propose that Süssmayr's involvement with the completion of the *Requiem* had nothing to do with an alleged romantic involvement with Constanze. Instead, the entire event might be looked at through a more innocent prism, one that uses the principle of Occam's razor, a rational axiom suggesting the selection of the simplest explanation for a sequence of events. It is a more formal way of expressing the idea found in the maxim, "Should you hear hoof beats on the plains, think horses, not zebras."

Constanze's first choice candidate to complete the *Requiem* probably was Süssmayr, given his alleged conversations with Mozart and his experience with the *Kyrie* fugue's completion. However, it has been suggested that each year, in about the middle of December, Süssmayr would go to Kremsmünster along with Pasterwitz to work on the Abbey's annual Christmas pageant. So, Constanze may have tried to approach Süssmayr, only to find that he was leaving for Kremsmünster and could not or would not change his plans. Alternatively, she might have found him already gone without notifying her. According to another unconfirmed report — which, when searched for, could not be found — the records of the Abbey are alleged to document both Süssmayr and Pasterwitz arriving in Kremsmünster on December 17, a date very much in harmony with the date of Constanze's suggested invitation to Eybler. That the two men were in Kremsmünster during the Christmas season of 1794 has been confirmed by an official of Kremsmünster Abbey, but proof that both were there in 1791 cannot be found. Süssmayr's hypothetical departure from Vienna on

December 13 is calculated under the assumption that the 104 miles between Vienna and Kremsmünster would have taken several days by coach in the Austrian winter.

If this is what happened, Constanze would have been quite put out. Some thirty-six years later, she remembered her anger but, perhaps, not the cause. Alternatively, she might not have wanted to speak either about Süssmayr or the cause of her anger. In certain of Mozart's letters, Süssmayr's name (as well as the names of others) was defaced, presumably at her request. The accusations that cast doubt on her faithfulness to Mozart may still have pained her even at a distance of thirty-six years. In any case, turning to Eybler around December 15, she received his agreement on December 21.

Constanze must have been devastated when Eybler suddenly withdrew from his agreement to complete the job. In Süssmayr's absence, Eybler had appeared to supply the answer to her urgent problem. Now, she was in trouble and time was slipping by. She therefore turned to various others, according to conventional wisdom, all of whom unidentified and all of them unable to provide assistance. Finally, going back to Süssmayr, who had returned to Vienna from Kremsmünster by that time, she got him to take on the task.

As for her last child bearing the name of Franz Xaver, the predilection to see only dark motives in that shows that a selective approach has been taken with respect to the question of Constanze's constancy. That her first child, Raimund (who died at the age of two months), was named after the banker Raimund Wetzlar has never produced any similar allegations. Besides, the name "Franz Xaver" was not uncommon at that time, as the family friend and Mozart biographer Franz Xaver Niemetschek demonstrates.

With Süssmayr's agreement to take on the task, Constanze must have felt a wave of relief. Little did she know the roadblocks that lay in wait for her.

Defining "Incomplete"

Since only one section of the Mozart *Requiem* can be performed as a finished composition exactly as written, the remainder of the work, approximately seventy manuscript surfaces, is by definition "incomplete," a word so imprecise that it allows the imagination to run in all directions, encouraging wide-ranging speculation. But precision of understanding about the ways in which the *Requiem* is incomplete is essential, for without it, the actions required to make the work performable may be misunderstood, or worse, assumed to be trivial.

Paradoxically, it is the profundity of Mozart's compositions that brings about this confusion, namely that almost any incomplete work of his should be naturally easy to finish. When we think of Beethoven's compositions, we envision a titan struggling with his creativity. He writes in such a rush that his manuscripts occasionally border on the unreadable. He scribbles and then defaces what he has scribbled. Ink splatters the page. He keeps notebooks, sketches, and fragments that he fills with ideas as he walks in woods to contemplate his muse. The romantic picture of Beethoven is that each composition that he completes is born only after months or even years of arduous labor accompanied by multiple revisions.

But when we picture Mozart composing, we think of him as a man whose creativity did not require combat with the gods; that is, his compositions are perceived — though erroneously — as flowing effortlessly from his head to his hand. Thus, in the context of a Mozart composition, some interpret "incomplete" as meaning that only a few minor details are required to finish it.

But these romantic pictures of creative genius are, in Mozart's case at least, a serious misunderstanding. The seemingly effortless often takes a great deal of sweat to accomplish, and Mozart's oeuvre is no exception, which makes most of the speculation about how easy it might have been to complete the unfinished *Requiem* tragically unrealistic. Complicating the history of the situation is the belief — outrageously exaggerated and getting worse with time — that, in some uncertain way, Mozart arranged, during his lifetime, for the work's completion by others after his death, and also, through notes and sketches, reached back from beyond the grave to help consummate the effort.

Considering the fact that the incompleteness of the Mozart *Requiem* is arguably the most studied problem in the history of music, it is essential to know some details about the state of the work at the time of the composer's death. Only then can we begin to appreciate the last two centuries of *Requiem* study as well as the work's transition from unfinished to concluded.

Not only is the *Requiem* incomplete, it has three different kinds of deficiencies, and each presents a unique set of problems. The first is the least serious of the three, though it is serious enough. It centers around the undeniable fact that, following the complete *Requiem aeternam*, Mozart drafted nine individual, self-contained compositions and eight of them, though architecturally whole, did not have sufficient orchestral accompaniment to allow a public performance.

In effect, what Mozart wrote down for eight of these nine incomplete sections are not compositions but blueprints for compositions. They might well have been totally finished in his head, requiring only the writing down of instrumental details at a later date. But whatever Mozart's intentions, these eight blueprinted sections were far too sketchy to allow us reliably to project exactly what the orchestral accompaniment would be when the works were performed. Understanding the possible solutions to this first dimension of the three fundamental *Requiem* problems requires knowledge, not of his elegant creative process, but of the mundane mechanics of how he wrote down his compositions.

The second dimension of incompleteness applies to only one section of the nine that follow the *Requiem aeternam*, namely, the *Lacrimosa*. Based on the breathtaking beginning of eight measures that Mozart laid out before he stopped work — two measures for strings and six for choral voices — one can safely state that it is a tragedy for all humanity that the magnificent promise is terminated so prematurely. While the problems of the first dimension can be repaired, those of the *Lacrimosa* are much more serious: so little music is present, and what is written has an uncertain architecture. It is not even long enough to be considered a work in progress; the eight measures inaugurate a beginning, but there is neither a middle nor an end. So, while eight of the nine unfinished sections theoretically could be completed, it is impossible to complete the *Lacrimosa* in any traditional sense. Instead, it must be created — and mostly from whole cloth — an awesome labor to ask of anyone, considering whose shoes have to be filled.

The task of reading between the lines of the eight sections that fall in the class of first-dimension problems may be compared to deciphering the blueprints of the composition's superstructure; but the *Lacrimosa* is a problem of a different magnitude. Here, the completer must try to understand what was intended for this section but with very little data to support a journey into Mozart's head. On the contrary, there is hard evidence that the *Lacrimosa*, and how to finish it, troubled even Mozart's stupendous musical intellect.

The third dimension of "incomplete" is the most complex and stressful of the three. One must come to grips with the fact that the Mozart *Requiem*, as written, is liturgically unsuitable because it is too short. Following the portion of the mass accompanied by Mozart's last written notes, there are further religious duties that must be undertaken before the task of the requiem mass is concluded and its purpose achieved. Without additional music, the work does not fully act as a suitable participant in the somber devotions of the religious moment. And, any music that might be added would have to be created from whole cloth since Mozart appears to have left no written clues as to how the work was to continue, though there is strong dispute with respect to this assertion. Finally, whatever music is to be added must also contain a stirring musical conclusion (as is required of any good composition), the purpose of which is to uplift the spirit while concluding the requiem mass with somber dignity.

Underlying any attempt to fix any of the three dimensions of the problem is the realization that the fixer is standing in for the man whom some consider to be the single greatest musical talent who ever lived, the very epitome of compositional elegance, sophistication, and technical excellence. It is enough to frighten off the bravest soul.

THE FIRST DIMENSION

Many composers, certainly including Mozart, create compositions in a highly individualized way, and in this I mean not the unfathomable mysteries of artistic creativity but the workaday task of writing notes on paper. It is the manner in which music traveled from Mozart's head to his hand that resulted in the first of the three problems enumerated above.

While it may seem logical to create the score of a composition from top to bottom, one instrument and a few measures at a time, it generally is not done that way. Mozart's creations did develop from left to right, but only for a few instruments (or voices) at a time. He would write some number of measures of music — perhaps even all of a particular section — for two instruments, or a solo vocal line and one instrument. Then, perhaps with several repetitions, he would go back to the beginning and add more instruments. The various instrumental layers that he created sometimes can be distinguished due to differences in the writing. Nor did the creation of another instrumental layer necessarily immediately follow its predecessor. For example, when he returned after a few minutes, hours, or days to add a new stratum of orchestration, random chance might result in his selecting a different bottle of ink, one with a noticeably dissimilar tint. Interestingly, that sometimes allows one to follow the sequence of the creative process.

The term "draft" is used to describe a creation in which the formal process of composition has been begun, but not completed. If Mozart were creating a multi-section composition — as is the *Requiem* — he might begin drafting one section and stay with it until the architecture was complete. However, even after it was structured, the work might still be unperformable because of the lack of detail for certain orchestral instruments. At this early stage, he might not even identify the names of all of the orchestral instruments.

Alternatively, Mozart might begin a draft and then encounter compositional difficulties that needed to be resolved. This could delay the various stages of the drafting process for that section. Or he might draft several independent sections in one go.

In the specific case of the *Requiem*, he did all kinds of things. The first section, the *Requiem aeternam*, is not a draft, though it went through such a stage on the way to becoming an almost entirely finished section. Of the next nine sections, eight are drafted to the point of architectural completion, though the orchestral writing was far from finished. Specifically, some of the instruments he probably intended to use are neither identified nor have any music written for them because he never got around to it, and he wrote hardly any music for some of the instruments that are explicitly identified. In some places, both conditions exist. Finally, one section, the *Lacrimosa*, is a draft of such brevity that even its architecture is uncertain and Mozart's intentions are quite unclear.

Of the eight sections with architecturally complete drafts, their imperfection does not necessarily mean that they were unfinished in Mozart's head; it only means that he died before getting to the details of completing the orchestration on music paper.

In the *Requiem*, Mozart had two kinds of movements to create — those with a chorus and orchestra, and those with one or more soloists and orchestra (which might also include choral participation). Unlike Handel's Messiah, for example, there are no purely orchestral sections in the *Requiem*.

For choral movements, he composed by first writing all the musical lines of the four choral voices (soprano, alto, tenor, and bass), along with the orchestral bass part which acted as a guide to the harmonic content of that section. Happily, all of the sections of the *Requiem* composed by Mozart — except the *Lacrimosa* — have the entirety of the vocal music present, from first note to last. In this way Mozart established the architecture and defined his harmonies.

As part of these choral movements, he might include a fragmentary tier for one or more orchestral instruments, sometimes a measure or two, sometimes more. It was there to remind him at a later time — or someone else, perhaps — of the kind of accompaniment he had in mind, so that the section could be completely fleshed out. For example, in only one of the eight structurally complete but still unperformable sections of the *Requiem* is the first violin part completely written out. In every other section, the music for the first violin is fragmentary. And in at least one other section, not a single note for second violin appears. But the fragmentary nature of the orchestral accompaniment notwithstanding, the critical ingredient was in place, that is, the writing of both the complete set of four vocal parts and the orchestral bass.

Each such section had a beginning, a middle, an end, a harmonic design contained in the choral parts and bass line, and perhaps some fragmentary orchestral passages as well, all written in his neat, clear, precise script. (His handwriting was invariably neat during the drafting process, but, as we shall see, when he sketched things, it was sometimes much more problematic.)

For sections with one or more vocal soloists, participating either one at a time or in ensemble, he might or might not include some instrumental lines. But the solo vocal lines and the critical instrumental bass line were invariably complete.

In effect, while this first dimension of the incompleteness of the Mozart *Requiem* shows how disappointing and frustrating it is to contemplate the piece in its final form, it still describes a situation that can be repaired. Given a competent musician with experience in writing for the orchestra, Mozart's structured choral parts, solo vocal lines, and orchestral bass act as blueprints that enable the movement to be completed by someone else. The sketchy instrumental lines also act as a guide to the character of the intended accompaniment, telling the finisher something about what Mozart's ideas were for the orchestral passages. However, no matter how competent the person who does the completion, and no matter how brilliantly that effort is made, it is certain that, to varying degrees, Mozart would have done it differently.

And that is not due to the musical superiority of one person over the other; any task that entails thousands of details and hundreds of decisions will be done differently by different individuals. Furthermore, if the person completing the section is not well trained or has insufficient experience, the work will almost certainly contain technical errors ranging from modest to significant.

The good news is that so many sections had enough of the architecture written down by Mozart to allow completion and make them performable. But even so, such completions by another hand do not constitute Mozart's work, though his ideas would, of course, be the seeds that germinate into the end product. The quality of completion is highly dependent on the skill of the completer.

THE FIRST DIMENSION: *Kyrie*

To summarize the condition of the *Requiem* at the moment of Mozart's death, a total of ten sections of the work existed, though the level of completion varied from section to section. Mozart himself completed the first, the *Requiem aeternam*, in almost all respects. Following that, were nine drafts or incomplete sections, eight of which, though architecturally complete, were unperformable as written. The first of those nine is that of a colossal fugue known as the *"Kyrie," "The Kyrie* fugue," or the *"Kyrie eleison."* The text, repeated many times, is quite brief.

> *Lord have mercy on us.*
> *Christ have mercy on us.*

The assertion that the *Kyrie* was an incomplete section of the *Requiem* at the time of Mozart's death will come as a surprise to those who believe that it, like the opening *Requiem aeternam,* was completed entirely by Mozart. Prior to the 1970s, few would have disputed that statement. But, like many things thought to be true of the *Requiem,* it was not; and for approximately 170 years, no one realized it.

Not until the German musicologist Franz Beyer examined the original manuscript in preparation for his work on a new edition of the *Requiem* and made a critical examination of the autograph did it become known that additional hands had been involved in some of the instrumental lines of the *Kyrie.* As it turns out, on the fifth day after Mozart's death, the first two sections of the *Requiem* are said to have been performed as part of a memorial service for the composer. This does not imply that the entire *Requiem* was performed on that date; that could not have happened, even though several unreliable contemporary news reports stated exactly that. In fact, only the first two sections were heard.

In the five-day period following his death, and as postulated from handwriting analysis, Mozart's incomplete draft of the *Kyrie* fugue is believed to have been completed by at least two and possibly three people. This tells us that knowledge of the *Requiem* being incomplete was known by at least a few people almost from the moment of Mozart's death.

What had passed unnoticed by everyone except Beyer was that the original manuscript of the *Kyrie* — stated to be completely in Mozart's hand in all the literature on the subject — had an abnormally high number of wrong notes for the two orchestral basset horns, something categorically foreign to Mozart's instrumental writing. It is not that he never made mistakes, but a high number of wrong notes for a specific instrument — one for which he had written with complete mastery on many occasions — was an event without precedent. And the reason no one had previously commented on this anomaly was because the incorrect notes appeared only in the original manuscript, with corrections having been made for printed editions. This eliminated any opportunity for most people to observe and ponder the abnormality.

Of course, whoever prepared the first printed edition using a copy of the manuscript of the *Kyrie* — the original owned by Wallsegg was not used — would have noticed these errors. But, beyond correcting the faulty transpositions, such a person would not necessarily have reacted to an anomaly of this nature. Perhaps their editorial skills might not have included the kinds of historical knowledge that would allow them to respond to such a significant abnormality. One must know a great deal about Mozart's music-writing habits to be able to recognize such an aberration when it arises.

Franz Beyer had those skills, and his discovery led him to examine the handwritings in the original manuscript of the *Kyrie* fugue more thoroughly than had ever been done previously. It was he who first rejected the hypothesis that this section of the *Requiem* was entirely in Mozart's hand. Now, and with the benefit of hindsight, other clues may be seen in the manuscript that demonstrate Mozart's noninvolvement with the complete instrumentation of the *Kyrie*. However, the first discovery of this almost lost piece of history was Beyer's alone.

In hindsight, it is easy to understand how everyone else missed the boat. Though a facsimile of the original manuscript has been available since 1913 (with several reprints issued after that time, as well as a far superior new one in 1991), a cursory examination of the first two sections would allow any reasonable person to conclude that both were completely in Mozart's hand. The music is all there. It is complete in every respect. The entire instrumentation is present. And if that were not enough to fool everyone, the handwriting looks deceptively like Mozart's; that is, at least until the abnormally high number of incorrectly transposed basset horn notes noticed by Beyer are given the consideration that they deserve. The fact that the wrong notes were for basset horns — a member of the clarinet family but pitched in a unique key — was revealing because the instrument's atypical pitch would be exactly the sort of thing that might trip up someone with lesser skills.

The *Requiem*'s first section, *Requiem aeternam*, ends with its single final measure appearing on the tenth surface of the manuscript. Immediately adjacent to that is the first measure of the *Kyrie* fugue. Including the surface on which it begins, a total of eight surfaces are required for the *Kyrie*. Thus, at this point of the composition, Mozart had used up seventeen of his 80 surfaces (plus some blanks).

Because the instrumental completion for the *Kyrie* fugue was done on the same paper that Mozart had used for his draft of that section, it is necessary to subtract out the music that appears not to be in Mozart's hand — a very difficult task — in order to speculate what might have been on the page at the moment of his death. Specifically, he appears to have written the four choral parts, the bass line, and, perhaps, some hints at an orchestration. The rest of the instrumentation was placed into Mozart's original manuscript by at least two people, one of whom, by the handwriting, has been identified as Süssmayr, who is said to have contributed at least the trumpet and timpani parts. The identification of the other hand(s) is still disputed.

The completion of the *Kyrie* fugue was an event totally unrelated to the completion of the entire *Requiem*, a task later undertaken but abandoned by Eybler, perhaps offered to but refused by others, and finally completed by Süssmayr. The *Kyrie* was completed neither for the same purpose nor on the same schedule as the remainder of the *Requiem*. It is thought to have been completed in the five days following Mozart's death, and is believed to have been performed, along with the *Requiem aeternam*, as part of a memorial service held on December 10, 1791 in Vienna's Church of St. Michael.

An important question that arises has to do with Count Wallsegg's knowledge of both the memorial service and the fact that a part of what was supposed to be his exclusive property was played at the event. If Wallsegg had an exclusivity agreement with Mozart — as is believed to be the case — he could well have been in a position to assert that the December 10 performance, even though of only two sections, violated that agreement. As we shall see, Constanze's multiple violations of what surely would have been part of a well-constructed contract eventually resulted in difficulties for her.

THE FIRST DIMENSION: *Dies Irae* to *Hostias*

The previous discussion on the *Kyrie* fugue spoke of the first of the nine sections left in draft form by Mozart; it was treated as a special case for three reasons. First, its completion was achieved separately from the larger task of producing a performable version of the entire *Requiem*. Second, the work to complete it seems to have been done by at least two people, one being Süssmayr and the other(s) not positively identified. Third, the fact that the *Kyrie* was a draft not completed by Mozart is sufficiently new information that it must receive special attention, at least in contrast with the other sections of the *Requiem*, all of which were later completed by Süssmayr.

Now, however, we put aside the matter of the *Kyrie* and focus on the state of the rest of the *Requiem*'s sections that were begun but not completed by Mozart. Eybler made completions of some of that music (*Dies irae, Tuba mirum, Rex tremendae, Recordare,* and *Confutatis*) right on Mozart's original manuscript. But his eventual abandonment of the task has relegated him to the wings as far as the history of the *Requiem*.

Until recently, Eybler's partial completion of the *Requiem* had almost no public exposure. Fortunately, thanks to the efforts of musicologist H.C. Robbins Landon, an edition and recording of

Eybler's effort (conjoined with some of Süssmayr's material) now exists. However, and until recently when a number of fresh reworkings of the *Requiem* were made, any performance of the work invariably meant Süssmayr's completion. This was because, for almost two centuries, his was the only one published.

A final point dealing with Eybler's involvement relates to his working method, which involved placing his additions directly onto the autograph itself, an act that corrupted the original manuscript. The exact point at which he stopped work occurs in the *Lacrimosa* where he added two measures of melodic continuation to the choral soprano part. While Süssmayr usurped some of Eybler's ideas, other parts of his completion are independent of it.

By the time that Süssmayr began his task, the original manuscript was so contaminated that he had to create an entirely new score. In fact, it is probably more complicated than that. He may have created a working score first and, on finishing it, copied it again, this time neatly, as would be expected of a presentation document. The story of the organization and content of the score that was presented to Wallsegg through his intermediary will be detailed later.

When this presentation score surfaced almost half a century after Wallsegg took possession of it, it was first believed to be entirely in Mozart's hand. However, the eventual realization that only parts of this document were written down by Mozart led to a great deal of confusion and a bizarre cover-up in which Austrian censors collaborated. Strangely, this peculiar and embarrassing event followed only a few years after damning claims from another quarter that the music known as the Mozart *Requiem* was entirely a forgery, that not one note of the work was by him, and that something of a crime had been perpetrated on the public at large.

For now, let us measure the extent of the deficiencies of all the sections following the *Kyrie* (except for the *Lacrimosa*) that were begun but not completed by Mozart. We begin with the *Dies irae*.

The day of wrath, that day
shall reduce the world to ashes
as David and the Sibyl testify.
How great the trembling shall be
when the Judge shall come
who sternly knows all things.

The *Dies irae* is sixty-two per cent unfinished. How that raw number is derived from the reality of the situation requires a detailed explanation.

The probable number of separate vocal and instrumental musical lines that Mozart would have had to write down in a finished *Dies irae* is assumed, on the basis of what was is present in the instrumentation of the *Requiem aeternam*, to be fifteen. That's eleven separate orchestral instruments, to be named in a moment, and four choral voices.

Each one of these fifteen threads would have required sixty-eight measures of music, which is the length of the *Dies irae*. What this says is that, had Mozart finished this section, he would have written a total of 1020 measures (fifteen lines of music multiplied by sixty-eight measures per line), with each measure containing music, silence, or a blend of both depending on the composer's intentions and the musical needs of the moment. However, the thread for the orchestral bass line also serves as music for two other instruments, the cello and the organ. Furthermore, the three trombones are duplications of the alto, tenor, and bass voices. While this brings the total number of separate instruments and voices up to twenty, we will still assume fifteen because our interest is in distinct lines of music that have to be created, not the number of distinct musical instruments.

Because the instruments Mozart intended to use for the *Dies irae* are barely identified, we need a precise description of how one gets to the definition of the fifteen threads. The only explicit instrumental or human voice descriptions present in the manuscript of the *Dies irae* and written by Mozart are the four choral parts and the orchestral bass thread, which, as mentioned, involves writing one thread that serves for three orchestral instruments.

We can make certain assumptions about which woodwinds, brasses, and percussion Mozart intended to use in this and all following sections. Mozart explicitly defines two basset horns, two bassoons, two trumpets, three trombones, and timpani in the *Requiem aeternam*. The trombones, strangely enough, are not identified until the seventh measure and both how many of them and what they are to play is not entirely clear. However, there is a good historical understanding and a tradition with respect to how trombones were used in church music of this period. Therefore, their presence as defined in the *Requiem aeternam* suggests their use in other sections, though not necessarily all at the same time. The brasses assist in supplying a variety of musical and emotional effects (glory, terror, etc.) and are typical for church music. They also had the practical advantage of adding heft in loud sections. And, it is inconceivable that Mozart would not have used a standard complement of strings, even if they are unspecified by name.

Consequently, using the instrumentation explicitly indicated for the *Requiem aeternam*, perhaps supplemented with hints and suggestions from Mozart before his death, it is not unreasonable to presume a specific instrumentation for the imposing needs of the *Dies irae*. It is a strong and forceful section, requiring a strong and forceful orchestra.

Mozart would have written music for his fifteen instrumental and human voices on twelve-stave paper in the following way. One stave would have been used for a pair of basset horns, another for a pair of bassoons, and a third for a pair of trumpets — writing for two instruments on one stave was common practice. A fourth stave would be reserved for the timpani. Thus four staves serve the need of seven instruments. Four additional staves would have been used for the first violin, second violin, viola, and orchestral bass, bringing the total to eight staves for eleven instruments. Finally, four staves would be used for the four voices of the chorus, the soprano, alto, tenor, and vocal bass. In this way, the twelve staves of the music paper would have been fully utilized and efficiently, too, for the eleven musical instruments and four choral voices. No additional staves would be needed for cello or organ because the orchestral bass line would be used for them as well as the bass.

As for the trombones, it appears that Mozart intended three of them to reinforce the alto, tenor, and bass choral voices in louder sections. That Mozart might have wanted a soprano trombone (also called "the slide trumpet") to reinforce the soprano choral voice is a complicated, controversial, and unresolved issue. But because trombones are assumed to play that which the chorus sings, that trombone music is inherently contained in the choral parts. Therefore, they do not require additional space in a score whose twelve staves per page were fully assigned. Further evidence of Mozart's intentions regarding the use of trombones appears later in the *Requiem* when a single trombone is given an extended solo passage in the *Tuba mirum*.

Deriving the unfinished percentage of the *Dies irae* is, from this point, a matter of arithmetic; that is, had he lived, Mozart would have written 1020 measures of music for the fifteen instrumental and human voices. It does not matter that all of the players would not have been playing or singing constantly throughout the 68 measures of the section. Decisions needed to be made about these instruments, and, even though one or more instrumentalists or singers might not participate at certain points, the decision to use or not use them is part of the process of orchestration, or writing for an orchestra.

So 1020 measures of music or silence would have had to be defined, created, and written down. Some of these measures might have had many notes, others few, and some could be left totally or partially empty because that voice or instrument was not being used at a particular moment. Of the 1020 measures needed for the *Dies irae*, Mozart wrote only 390. These comprise the complete set of four choral parts of 272 measures (four vocal threads at 68 measures per thread), the entire bass line (68 measures), 42 measures of first violin music, and four each for second violin and viola. Nothing in

Mozart's hand is present or even suggested for basset horns, bassoons, trumpets, trombones, or timpani.

Whoever was to complete this section would have to make decisions about 630 measures of music or silence — that's 1020 measures needed for the section minus the 390 measures contributed by Mozart. Thus, the *Dies irae* is 630 measures unfinished, 62 per cent incomplete — although that sounds worse than it really is. A missing first violin part would be terrible, but a missing trumpet part is less critical. The work of the completer was to assess each section, deduce the needed instrumental contributions for that section, and then create them.

For the *Dies irae*, Mozart used ten surfaces of paper. This brings the running surface count of the original manuscript to 27 used of the 80 present.

The *Tuba mirum* represents a different problem of orchestration because it is the first calm moment since the opening *Requiem aeternam*. The desired orchestral texture is presumed to call for a smaller group of players. Trumpets or timpani were almost certainly not intended, though Mozart explicitly requests a solo trombone. Because this section is made up almost entirely of solo vocal passages, it requires skillful management of the orchestral resources so as not to overwhelm the singers. The text of the section reads:

> The trumpet, sending its wondrous sound
> through the sepulchers in every land,
> shall gather all before the throne,
> death and nature will be brought forth
> when all creatures shall rise again
> to answer the Judge.
> The written Book will be brought forth
> in which all is contained,
> whence the world is to be judged.
> When therefore the Judge will be seated,
> whatever is hidden shall appear,
> no wrong will remain unpunished.
> What patron shall I entreat
> when even the just man is scarcely safe?

The *Tuba mirum*, 62 measures long, is for four solo voices which sing consecutively and separately for a total of fifty measures, with each vocal entrance except the first terminating the singing of its predecessor. For the final twelve measures, the four voices join together in ensemble. All vocal parts are present as is the orchestral bass. Neither basset horns nor bassoons are indicated though it is presumed that Mozart intended them for use. Thus all 62 measures for the four wind instruments must be supplied by the completer.

There is only one trombone present; the others are presumed to be excluded. The tenor trombone's solo music is written out completely by Mozart for eighteen measures but there is no indication of what the player should do beyond that point. Only nineteen measures of first violin are present, one measure of second violin, and no measures for the viola are indicated.

Taking everything into consideration, a total of 806 measure choices need to be made of which only 348 were given by Mozart. Thus, the movement can be characterized as 57 per cent incomplete. Eight surfaces of paper are used for the *Tuba Mirum*, bringing the running total to 35 of 80 surfaces.

The *Rex tremendae*, returns us to a strong and orchestrally forceful choral movement, though brief, being only 22 measures long.

> *King of tremendous majesty!*
> *Who saves freely those to be saved.*
> *Save me, O fount of mercy!*

Using the same methodology as was employed for earlier sections, the *Rex tremendae* is suggested to be 60 per cent incomplete. Five surfaces of paper are used for the *Rex tremendae*, bringing the running total to 40 of 80 surfaces.

The *Recordare* is a long, contemplative movement of 130 measures for solo voices, a pair of basset horns explicitly indicated, and a presumption of both a bassoon pair and standard orchestral strings. By the same analysis, it is suggested that this section is 54 per cent incomplete. Thirteen surfaces of paper are required for the *Recordare*, which results in 53 of 80 having been used thus far.

> *Remember, sweet Jesus,*
> *I am the cause of your coming.*
> *Do not abandon me on that day.*
> *You sat down weary as you searched for me;*
> *You suffered the Cross to redeem me;*
> *Let not such pains be vain.*
> *Fair judge of vengeance,*
> *Make the gift of absolution*
> *Before the day of reckoning.*
> *I groan like an accused,*
> *I blush with guilt.*
> *Spare me, O Lord, I beg you.*
> *You absolved Mary,*
> *You heard out the thief,*
> *To me as well you gave hope.*
> *Have mercy on me,*
> *But you are good.*
> *Let me not be burned in eternal fire.*
> *Let me have a place among the sheep.*
> *Set me apart from the goats*
> *Set me on your right hand.*

The *Confutatis* is forty measures long, sixty per cent unfinished, and uses seven surfaces of paper bringing the running total to sixty of 80 surfaces.

> *When the wicked have been confounded*
> *And cast into the devouring flames,*
> *Call me with the blessed!*
> *I pray suppliant and kneeling,*
> *My heart is crushed as to ashes*
> *Watch over my final hour.*

Following the *Confutatis* is the *Lacrimosa*, which will be dealt with in due course. However, only two surfaces of paper are used for the section, bringing the running total to 62 of 80.

The *Domine Jesu/Quam olim* that follows the *Lacrimosa* is 78 measures long and 56 per cent incomplete. It requires thirteen surfaces to write down, bringing the running total to 75 of 80 surfaces.

> *Lord, Jesus Christ, king of glory,*
> *Free the souls of all the faithful departed*
> *From punishments of Hell and the deep lake;*
> *Free them from the lion's mouth,*
> *And let not Tartarus suck them in,*
> *Let them not fall into the dark*
> *but let your standard-bearer, St. Michael,*
> *Lead them into the holy light:*
> *[Quam olim Abrahae]*
> *Which once Thou didst promise to Abraham*
> *And to his seed.*

The final section in Mozart's manuscript, the *Hostias/Quam olim*, is 54 measures long plus 35 additional measures that exactly repeat the *Quam olim Abrahae* fugue, heard previously as the final 35 measures of the *Domine Jesu/Quam olim*. Not including the recapitulated section (whose completion would have already been made by the time it was needed for the *Hostias*), the section is 55 per cent incomplete and requires five surfaces of paper, bringing the running total to 80, that being the end of the manuscript in Mozart's hand.

> *This sacrifice of prayer and praise, O Lord,*
> *do we offer to You.*
> *Accept it for the souls of these*
> *whom today we recall to memory.*
> *Grant, O Lord, that they may pass over*
> *from death to life:*
> *[Quam olim Abrahae]*
> *Which once Thou didst promise to Abraham*
> *And to his seed.*

Given the state of completion of the sections described above — a total of seven excluding the *Kyrie* and the *Lacrimosa* — one could ask how long it would take a competent arranger to bring the material to completion. The answer might appear to be inversely related to the expertise of the completer; that is, the greater the competence of the arranger, the shorter the time. However, in my opinion, the answer is exactly the opposite. Specifically, the weaker arranger will take much less time than the expert precisely because he does not know enough to spend the additional time needed to do it properly. Furthermore, that person is capable of making severe errors if he is unaware of stylistic considerations for religious music of this period.

So a more responsible answer to the question might be that a less experienced person could probably do the work for those six sections in two to three months. A more experienced person would be likely to take longer.

When Constanze first requested Eybler to complete the *Requiem*, he agreed on December 21, 1791 to finish the work "by the middle of the coming Lent." Since the Lenten season of that year began on February 22, 1792, with Easter falling April 8, 1792, what Eybler had agreed to do was to finish the *Requiem* by around the middle of March. That would be a reasonable estimate for the completion of the movements that Mozart left in draft form, but a serious underestimation of the time needed for the entire task including writing the additional sections that had to be composed from scratch. Perhaps when he fully understood the magnitude of the job, Eybler realized that he could not complete it within his estimated timeframe, and that may have been the reason why he withdrew.

Considering that he could presumably not expect to be paid for doing this work for Constanze, and considering that it might occupy him for twice as long as he originally had thought, his decision to withdraw is quite understandable. But it was a mistake — he could have become immortal. Instead, he relegated himself to a footnote in the history of the Mozart *Requiem*.

THE SECOND DIMENSION

Of the ten sections of the *Requiem* that appear in whole or in part in Mozart's own hand, only one is so deficient in architecture that it cannot be completed, at least not in the same sense as the eight discussed previously. This section of the work contains insufficient material to allow that kind of completion; it is without architecture and is very much undefined. As such, it has to be almost totally composed, though Mozart drafted its brief front end.

That front end contains eight measures of music — an exquisite and breathtaking beginning for a conception of awesome power. However, at the same time, it is tragic precisely because it commences with such elegant promise and then...it breaks off.

After two measures of strings playing a figure designed to simulate the falling of tears, the chorus begins almost at a whisper, and then, as the music of a dramatic and extended ascending scale grows louder, the emotions become stronger and stronger until suddenly...it breaks off.

What caused Mozart to terminate the section so abruptly at this point? The romantic view is that, on writing the final notes of the eighth measure, he died — a perfect movie ending. So strong was this belief (and it remains so today) that a remark to that effect, as written by Joseph Eybler, appears on that page of the manuscript, declaring explicitly that these were Mozart's final notes. It is a lovely story that can break your heart, though it is almost certainly not true.

While it is possible, of course, it isn't probable. Two sections, the *Domine Jesu/Quam olim* and *Hostias/Quam olim*, both architecturally complete though without fully defined orchestral accompaniment, follow the *Lacrimosa* in the manuscript. Thus, to suggest that Mozart wrote the two final sections and then went back to begin but not finish the *Lacrimosa* is to describe a sequence of events foreign to Mozart's working habits. This non-normative procedure suggests something else entirely and forces the question, "What might have caused Mozart to stop composing after only eight measures?"

The most likely answer to that question is that he had not yet fully built the architecture for the *Lacrimosa* in his head. And until he had that structure fixed in his mind, he deliberately chose not to continue.

In order to lay out this section — that is, to create its

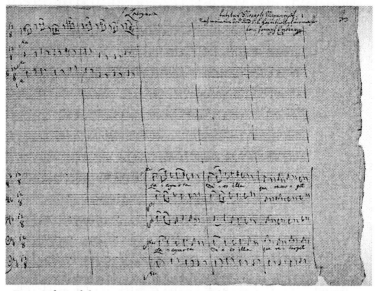

First surface of the *Lacrimosa* manuscript. Eybler's text in upper right corner states this music to be the last Mozart ever wrote, though the assertion is questionable.

architecture — Mozart had to come to grips with three issues: how should he begin, how should he end, and by what path would he go from the one to the other? While his beginning was sure-footed, I suggest that he had not yet reached a decision on how the *Lacrimosa* was going to be concluded. Without a better understanding of the as yet undefined end, he could not complete his beginning and construct a middle.

What evidence supports the assertion that Mozart's uncertainty about how he would end the *Lacrimosa* caused the sudden, premature, and (what the dying man may have thought of as temporary) break in the work? The answer is the presence of the word "Amen," as found in a partly readable sketch that has been in the Berlin State Library since the late nineteenth century. However, its relationship to the *Requiem* was not known until the 1960s.

In the 1960s, the German musicologist Wolfgang Plath examined this single sheet of paper written in Mozart's casual and occasionally unreadable sketch hand. On initial examination, there does not appear to be anything on this page that would allow one to relate it to the *Requiem*. Instead, the music requires the establishment of a sequence of interlocking observations, hypotheses, and logical conjectures before any theory can be arrived at concerning what the music is and where, in the body of Mozart's compositions, its placement was destined. Furthermore, only someone possessing considerable technical skill and an incredible breadth of knowledge about Mozart's music could have wended his way through those logical connections.

Plath's logic may be summarized as follows, though it is given as an imagined series of personal ruminations consisting of the kinds of typical inquiries and staged conclusions that are not uncommon in such situations. While the completely invented resolution shown here is swift, this is the kind of musicological problem that can take a long time to solve.

His musings would have begun with the simplest of questions: "What is this thing I am looking at?"

Then he would have continued with a series of initially obvious observations followed by a collection of far less evident conclusions:

This is a sheet of paper with ten staves on both sides, but sketch material is written only on one side. The other side has nothing but blank preprinted staves. On the side with music, the first two staves contain two separate sketches, cheek by jowl. The first item, consisting of four measures plus one note, appears to be a first try at the development section of *The Magic Flute* overture. The other sketch, also four measures plus one note, is not known to me, though that doesn't matter. The fact that the first of the

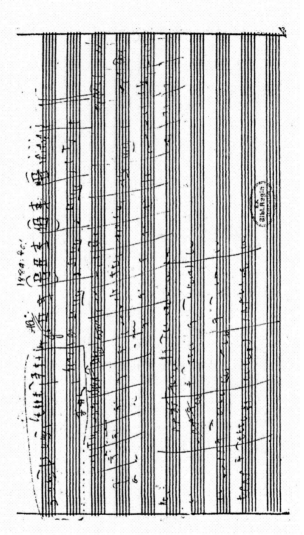

Sketch leaf containing the "Amen" Fugue

two sketches is from his penultimate opera dates the page to 1791, the year when he wrote that work.

Below *The Magic Flute* music are sixteen measures written on three staves for measures 1-12, and which expand to four staves for measures 13-16. Some of what is written is indecipherable. The scribbled word "Amen" appears twice, once on the upper voice and then, still as one word, spread out over seven measures for the second voice. I don't recognize this music. What it is, and to what composition it belongs, I do not know.

Because of the presence of the two words, both "Amen," this appears to be vocal music from a religious work, probably a choral part. I'll assume that this is a sketch for the four voices of a chorus. There are no clefs present, but if one presumes the clefs corresponding to the four staves are, from top to bottom, the soprano, alto, tenor, and bass clefs, then the piece appears to make sense only if the key signature has one flat. That would mean the work is in F major... Stop! That's a mistake. Let me rethink that conclusion... The music is in minor mode, not major; so that means the sketch is not in F major but rather D minor.

Well, since this piece of paper is from 1791, and this at times unreadable sketch is in the key of D minor, the question that must be asked is, "What works did Mozart write in that key in 1791?" There is only one... the Requiem.

So this sketch may have something to do with the *Requiem*. But what, and where might it belong? Why does the music of the sketch resemble nothing from the *Requiem*? Wait a moment... It is not entirely correct to state that it resembles nothing from the *Requiem*. In fact, though it is not an exact duplication, the first five or six notes of the melody bear a resemblance to the main theme of the *Requiem aeternam*, but upside down. That does not necessarily imply that the similarity was deliberate. It could have been a fortuitous accident or Mozart's subconscious at work. Could this music be something that was under consideration for use somewhere in the *Requiem*?

The music appears to be the sketch of a fugue. The two voices, in the soprano and alto clefs, singing the word "Amen," enter one after the other in fugal fashion. And two other voices also enter in fugal fashion, though without any text. Let me look harder. Are there any words other than "Amen"? ... No, there do not appear to be.

Let me think a moment ... Where does the word "Amen" appear in the Requiem? ... Of course! It does appear, but only once, namely as the last word heard in the Lacrimosa. It is amazing that a word so important to worship should appear only once in an extended religious service.

So, what this sketch appears to be is an attempt at creating a fugal conclusion of the *Lacrimosa* based on the word "Amen," because the *Requiem* is the only work he wrote in 1791 to which this sketch could possibly apply. But why a fugal conclusion? Why not a simple plagal cadence such as the one that Süssmayr used to end the *Lacrimosa*? Could it be that Mozart was considering an impressive fugal conclusion to the section?

The Catholic mass has distinct formal sections and the *Lacrimosa* ends one of them. The others all have impressive fugal conclusions so it is logical that this section should have one, too. Was that what was troubling Mozart? Was that why he had not concluded on how he would end the *Lacrimosa*? Is that why the manuscript draft of that tragic section breaks off after only eight measures?

Then, why didn't Süssmayr use this sketch and end the section as Mozart might have intended? There are three possible reasons.

First, he might not have seen it or known about it.

Second, if he did know of it, he might not have gone through the reasoning that would allow him to conclude what this thing was. The determination of what this sketch is and where it belongs is far from obvious.

Third, if he did see it, and did comprehend its purpose, did he have the required technical skill that would enable him to create a fugue of the necessary proportions? Maybe. Maybe not. We'll never know.

Whatever the reason, he didn't do it, and used instead the simpler solution of a two-chord plagal cadence, one chord on the syllable "A-" and a second chord on the syllable "-men." It's nice. It's served its purpose for two centuries; but is it what Mozart intended?

Now, leaving Plath's imagined ruminations, we return to reality to report that, subsequent to its discovery, at least three musicians have composed complete fugues based on the Amen sketch and intended for use as a conclusion of the Lacrimosa. One is Duncan Druce, another is Robert Levin, and a third is Richard Maunder. Perhaps others completions exist as responses to the enormous technical challenge posed by the sketch's brevity. But the completions of Druce, Levin, and Maunder have been incorporated into reworkings and recompletions of the entire *Requiem*, and all have been recorded, a subject that will be dealt with under the title, "Modern Day Süssmayrs."

It is also noted that a fourth item appears on the sketch sheet in question, though it is from another section of the *Requiem*, specifically the *Rex tremendae*. However, the presence of this sketch does not mean that the one above it — the one with the "Amen" text — it is also from the *Requiem*. That middle sketch really did require the kind of imagined ruminations described above, which is presented to demonstrate the level of knowledge and sophistication that one must have to reach conclusions about the purpose and intent of sketch material of otherwise uncertain intention.

Including Süssmayr's solution to the problem of how to complete the section, there are now at least four distinct versions of the *Lacrimosa*, each one an honest effort at solving the enormously difficult problem of building a house with the first brick — but nothing else — having been laid by Mozart. It is a revelation to see how each of these composers has put a different kind of "Amen" roof on the house.

SÜSSMAYR A PLAGIARIST? AN AMANUENSIS?

Was Süssmayr a plagiarist? That is a terrible insinuation that relates specifically to four sections of the *Requiem*, only one of which we have discussed in any detail thus far. Those four sections are all of the (1) *Sanctus/Osanna*, (2) *Benedictus/Osanna*, and (3) *Agnus Dei*, whose details will be reviewed in the section, "Third Dimension," and (4) all but the first eight measures of the *Lacrimosa*, discussed in the previous section. Süssmayr said he composed them and he claimed unconditional authorship for them. The issue cannot be ignored and it requires a discussion of considerable breadth.

Strong suspicions have long been voiced about the origin of those sections; perhaps the great Mozart scholar, Alfred Einstein, said it most gently, in the 1937 essay whose title this book has borrowed, when he suggested that Süssmayr may have "dressed himself in plumage not his own." Distinguished scholars have stated this hypothesis strongly in the past and continue to do so today. The allegations are based on one or more of the following distinct perspectives:

First, some contend that the discussion(s) Süssmayr is said to have had with Mozart as he lay on his deathbed were substantive, and that during these discussions Mozart, verbally or otherwise, provided guidance of an unknown nature, which Süssmayr would later crystallize and incorporate into the sections under discussion. As a consequence, it is suggested that Süssmayr swore falsely when he claimed sole authorship of that material.

Second, Constanze Mozart is said to have given Süssmayr some uncertain material (allegedly referred to by her as "scraps") that were somehow related to the *Requiem*, which he may have used to create the sections of the *Requiem* attributed to him; and he said nothing about having done these things.

Third, the sections in question are said to be of too high quality to have been composed by Süssmayr; in other words, they are so good that it is assumed that only Mozart could have composed them.

Fourth, melodic material found in the sections attributed to Mozart is also found in the sections that Süssmayr said he alone wrote.

Because this last argument is objective, has been raised by distinguished scholars, and with evidence in support of their assertion, it deserves the most serious consideration.

Though all four arguments are important, they do not have the same weight. No existing evidence supports the first two claims, while the third represents opinion. But the fourth and final argument is chilling in its substance, because of its apparent objectivity and the well-deserved world-class reputations of the men who have mooted it.

This discussion of authorship will be discussed in several sections. The first, "Amanuensis," contrasts a perception of the role of a musical secretary with the reality of those duties, and it also suggests reasons why such grave allegations impugning Süssmayr's honesty are made. The second, "Scraps of Paper," examines the matter of what Constanze is alleged to have given to Süssmayr. The third, "Too Good for Süssmayr," looks at the value of subjective criticism in general as well as the worth of this specific argument. The fourth, "Tune Duplication," deals with the matter of similar melodies that exist between the Mozart and Süssmayr sections of the *Requiem*, and what conclusions may be drawn from this phenomenon. The fifth, "The Lesser Talent," inquires about the apparent anomaly of a brilliant composition produced by a supposedly minor talent.

In the movie *Amadeus* an invented, brief, but riveting scene occurs shortly before the fictional Mozart expires. As he lies on his deathbed, pale, with a weak voice, almost *in extremis*, Mozart dictates much of the *Requiem*'s *Confutatis*, not to Süssmayr but to Antonio Salieri, a real-life acquaintance presented in the movie as a mortal enemy. It is Salieri who acts in the capacity of an amanuensis, or a taker of musical dictation, in the entirely fictitious and fanciful scene.

The powerful moment shows Mozart creating the elements of the *Confutatis* in his head. His expression suddenly goes blank. He stares into space. And the dramatic intention is to show that the details of the *Confutatis* are falling into place in his head as if they were tumblers on a correctly dialed combination lock. Then, by singing in the weak voice of a dying man, he feeds fragments of his ideas to Salieri. In the space of a few minutes, not only does the amanuensis comprehend the rhythm, instrumentation, and occasionally problematic pitch of the given notes, but expands on them to write whole passages down.

Mozart, relentless in his impatience, rushes through measure after measure, sometimes making nonspecific requests and allowing Salieri hardly any time at all. He asks angrily, "Do you *have* it?" Salieri responds, "Not so fast. You are going too fast!" Mozart, more impatiently, inquires again, "Do you *have* it?!" Finally, Salieri, scribbling furiously, says, "Yes, I have it." In this frantic and stressful way, Salieri documents much of the architecture of that brief but imposing section of the *Requiem*.

It is a clever scene, showing how the various musical layers of the *Confutatis* compound and reinforce the terror spoken of in the sung text. Naturally, time considerations of the movie require that the scene be wrapped up quickly, thus compressing the drama and heightening the tension. So, from start to finish, a significant portion of the *Confutatis* takes only a few minutes of real time for Mozart to create and Salieri to write down.

The main problem with the scene is not that the wrong characters are involved, or that a draft section of the *Confutatis* is being written down by someone other than Mozart when, in fact, a draft of that section exists entirely in his hand. What is even more important is that the scene gives the blindingly false impression that this is the way and the speed at which an amanuensis works. Further, the drama gives the amanuensis a level of creative participation far beyond the act of taking musical dictation.

Strangely, while everyone knows that the drama was false historically, there was almost no criticism of the scene's inference that an amanuensis could work and actually be productive under such impossible circumstances and frenzied conditions. Thus, people might have come away from that scene with the idea that any real collaboration between Mozart and Süssmayr could have taken place in a not dissimilar way.

The subject here is what, and how much, under conditions of reality, Mozart might have been able to tell Süssmayr about how to finish the *Requiem*.

According to Süssmayr, he and Mozart "often" sang and played movements of the *Requiem*. He also said that Mozart "frequently" told him about the details of the composition and even described the instrumentation of the work. That information is unquantified and extremely vague. "Often" and "frequent" are casual terms and leave us with no idea of how many times and in what level of detail the two might have spoken.

It is in the absence of such specificity that the imagination runs rampant. And since we want the *Requiem* to be entirely by Mozart, we naturally assume that many conversations took place, with Mozart verbally transmitting a great deal of detailed information to Süssmayr. But the facts of Mozart's final illness argue strongly against the validity of such an imagined scenario.

In 1799, Constanze also made statements about Süssmayr and Mozart working together, specifically referencing the time of their collaboration as the moment when Mozart "saw that his death was upon him." And, in 1827 she confirmed Süssmayr's claim about singing the work with the weakening Mozart, though both of her remarks must be greeted skeptically. Almost everything she said about the *Requiem* and its completion was self-serving, and some of it was deliberately deceptive. She was strongly motivated — practically compelled — to supply a Mozart composition to Wallsegg's agent; a composition drafted by her husband but completed and expanded on by another party would not fit the bill. All of her statements have to be gauged in that light.

The evidence shows that she was committed to perpetrating a fraud on Wallsegg, though she may not have thought of it in that sense. Her continued exaggerations and outright falsifications about so many of the *Requiem*'s circumstances have fostered most of the confusion surrounding the work.

Even though Süssmayr is a different case entirely, there are problems with what he said, too. If, as we are led to believe, his conversations with Mozart took place during the final week of the composer's life, then the ability of Mozart to communicate effectively, with any level of detail, is very much in question.

Exactly what Mozart may have told Süssmayr is something we will never know. It is not even useful to speculate. Instead, we must consider the process of how music is transferred from the mind of one man to the hand of another, something that *Requiem* lovers may not have thought about in detail. Yet knowing how an amanuensis works is central to understanding Süssmayr's completion.

To help put the matter in some perspective, an examination of a similar situation from another moment of real-life music history is undertaken. We move forward into the twentieth century and the blind and paralyzed composer Frederic Delius. From 1928 until 1934, the English musician Eric Fenby lived much of the time in Delius' home in Grez-sur-Long, France. He was there to act in the same capacity of an amanuensis for Delius that Salieri fictionally performed for Mozart in the film *Amadeus*, and that Süssmayr is imagined to have done for Mozart in real life. Though Delius was paralyzed, he could speak, and Fenby acted as the pen that put to paper the music Delius had inside his head. Both men were skilled musicians and there should have been no difficulty in the conveying and understanding of musical ideas.

Over a working period of between six and seven years, much of it continuous, Fenby acted as an amanuensis for Delius' creation of nine works: *Song of Summer, Songs of Farewell, Fantastic Dance, A Late Lark*, the third violin *Sonata, Caprice, Elegy for cello, Irmelin Prelude*, and *Idyll*. That is an average of eight to twelve months of work for each completed manuscript. Such a range does not, of course, take into consideration factors such as score complexity, including instrumentation. Delius' works were probably instrumentally more complicated than Mozart's, but, even so, this comparison gives some idea of the realities of the situation. None of Delius' compositions is exceptionally long but the process of creating them was agonizingly slow and complicated because that is the nature of the task. There is a great deal of detail to communicate and it depends to no small degree on the personalities of the composer and the amanuensis. Over the period of their collaboration, Fenby would be required to ask thousands of questions to clarify Delius' halting, occasionally angry, and frequently insufficiently-detailed musical descriptions.

What this similar historical moment tells us is to be skeptical of any claim that Mozart, in the final week of his life, desperately ill, unconscious on occasion and irrational at times, would have been capable of transmitting anything but the most broad-brush ideas to Süssmayr. This is the moment when he might have suggested that

Süssmayr create the last two sections of the *Requiem* by duplicating the first two with changed text (as Constanze said, though Süssmayr contradicts her account with a different story). Here is where Mozart might have described specific instrumentation for the drafted sections, or the addition of a *Sanctus*, a *Benedictus*, and an *Agnus Dei*, telling Süssmayr that he would be obliged to compose those sections himself, perhaps even speaking in general terms about their content. But that he gave Süssmayr details of any kind beyond such an overview simply cannot pass any test of reason.

The man was half dead already. It was difficult to stay in the room with him because his body exuded such a foul odor. As his illness progressed, he became ever more feeble, barely able to sit up, and often lost consciousness. His arms and legs were enormously swollen and sensitive. His mind wandered. Yet, serious people have offered arguments about the construction of the *Requiem* that would have one believe that Mozart gave, or perhaps even dictated, specific compositional details of the sections of the *Requiem* for which Süssmayr claimed sole authorship.

To be blunt, such assertions are simply not credible. If Süssmayr received any specific instructions from Mozart about the completion of the *Requiem* — or, more to the point, the completion of the *Lacrimosa* and the creation of the sections to be discussed in "Third Dimension" — it is highly unlikely that he received the information this way.

At most, one week is about all the time that they might have had together, and even then it requires us to assume that the two did nothing but work night and day. In fact, their productive time would have been severely limited because of Mozart's continually and rapidly increasing incapacity. Contrast that with the six to seven years required for Fenby to write down Delius' nine compositions. Further, Mozart would not have been motivated to tell Süssmayr anything about the *Requiem* before he was sure he was dying (presuming that he knew this to be the case, which is highly questionable). Thus, any substantive conversations could only have begun (even in theory) in his final week.

One must ask why music lovers feel such a desperate need to believe that the hand of Mozart is everywhere in the *Requiem* while the hand of Süssmayr, as a creative artist, is nowhere. It is a personal matter, one that I suggest deals with the human need to believe in a just, kind universe, one in which things come out right in the end. For Mozart to die and leave his final, glorious work unfinished suggests that life is unfair; it is one of the most poignant dramas in human experience for an individual to die at the moment when the achievement of his greatest accomplishment is just in sight. The human need for comfort, the willingness to believe in anything that seems to bolster the chance for a happy ending, turns us away from rational acceptance of what probably happened.

Therefore, the popular view prefers to think that Mozart must have finished the work. He did so by telling Süssmayr all the really important things that needed to be done, and in considerable specificity.

In this way, what Süssmayr must have done is demoted to a clerical function of no creative importance. As long as his work can be seen to have been guided by Mozart's directions in his last few lucid moments, then the world's stability is retained.

With Mozart in charge, and not Süssmayr, "God is in his heaven and all's right with the world." There is almost an element of theological necessity to believe that things went that way.

SCRAPS OF PAPER

Throughout the *Requiem* literature, one finds references to "scraps" of paper that Constanze allegedly gave to Süssmayr. From those repeated assertions, many assumptions have been made about what those "scraps" could have contained and in what ways Süssmayr might have used them. The most commonly heard notion is that they might have been elements to be used in the construction of those *Requiem* sections for which Süssmayr later claimed full credit of authorship. Perhaps the most egregious use of the topic is found in the popular literature, such as program notes for both concerts and recordings, and some book reviews. There, assertions about the "scraps" have made the journey from cautious optimism through wishful thinking to the invention of theories about the "almost-certain" existence of considerable source material that Süssmayr must have had and used, without admitting their extent .

Were it known for certain that Süssmayr had access to and used Mozart source material beyond that of the unfinished manuscript score, this would be extraordinarily important information. If Constanze provided him with *Requiem* "scraps" to be used at any appropriate point in his creation of the completion, it would constitute evidence that Mozart's contribution to the project continued posthumously, thus further diminishing Süssmayr's role and magnifying Mozart's.

It was for this reason that, when the fugue sketch spoken of in "*Second Dimension*" was interpreted as being the nucleus of music that Mozart was considering for use in the *Lacrimosa*, the sketch was offered as corroboration of Constanze's alleged statement about scraps of paper. But it went far beyond corroboration. It was argued that, given the existence of one sketch, there was a likelihood that more such material must have existed. However, it is not rational to conclude that, "If one thing is found, there must another like it."

Because of the importance of Constanze's alleged statement, one must look at its source. Exactly what did she say? How reliable is it, taken in both its entirety and context? First, let's set the stage for bringing Constanze's alleged quote into the picture.

The *Requiem* ran into serious trouble in 1825. Assertions were made that the *Requiem* was "scarcely worthy to be called Mozart's work at all." Nor were the criticisms casual. Serious doubt was cast on Mozart's authorship of the entire score and one critic went so far as to suggest not only that nothing in the piece was by Mozart, but that a fraud had been perpetrated on the public.

In response to the charges, Maximilian Stadler, a family friend (and no relation to Mozart's contemporary clarinetist, Anton Stadler), defended the authenticity of the work in print. It is in his

1826 justification of the *Requiem*'s authorship that one finds the "scraps" of paper statement attributed to Constanze.

Abbé Maximilian Johann Karl Dominik Stadler (1748-1833) was an Austrian priest and musician, eight years older than Mozart. He was already acquainted with the composer by 1781, when the two played several of Mozart's violin sonatas together. Since each man played both violin and piano, when they made music together either could have played the one instrument or the other. A much later report offers the intriguing idea that Mozart played the violin part, though not on a violin. Instead it is suggested that he played it on a second piano.

However, until Mozart's death, the relationship between Stadler and the Mozart family was casual. It was after Mozart's passing that Stadler became a confidante of Constanze. He is credited with completing a number of Mozart fragments and preparing a catalog of Mozart's compositions. He may even have been one of the individuals Constanze asked to complete the *Requiem*. Stadler acted as Constanze's musical advisor and it is likely that most technical statements alleged to have been made by her about the *Requiem* (for example, a list of wrong notes she sent to the publisher Breitkopf & Härtel), were actually prepared by Stadler.

In his *Requiem* defense, Stadler wrote the following: "[Constanze] told me that a few scraps of paper with music on them were found on Mozart's desk after his death, which she had given to Herr Süssmayr. What they contained, and what use Süssmayr made of them, she did not know."

Here, the key word used by Stadler is the diminutive form of the German word "*Zettel*," namely "*Zettelchen*." It can mean a scrap or slip of paper, a note written on paper, or even paper alone. But since the most common translation of the word in almost all the English-language material on the Mozart *Requiem* is "scrap," this is going to be our first perspective of its meaning.

I suggest that Stadler's statement quoted above presents serious difficulties, some of which transcend the statement itself. The first problem is that the statement is hearsay. What Constanze

Abbé Maximilian Stadler

may have said is one thing. What Stadler said she said could be quite another.

Second, the finding of unspecified music on Mozart's desk after his death does not necessarily mean that it was related to the *Requiem*. The music could have belonged to any one of many other compositions.

Third, even if Constanze gave something to Süssmayr, the contents of these scraps were, by Stadler's own admission, unknown to her.

Fourth, there is no proof that Süssmayr, if he received such material, could recognize any significance they might have had, or find a way to use them.

Fifth, even if all the elements of the statement are true, there were not many scraps of paper, just "a few."

But the technical problems with Constanze's alleged statement run even deeper. Do we accept the use of the word "scraps" literally and proceed from that premise, or must we reinterpret what she is claimed to have said in order to achieve something more productive, and then advance from that perspective?

The term "scraps" leads to unresolvable complexities. For one thing, a scrap of paper has no particular definition. How big is a scrap — is it the size of a postage stamp or a bookmark? Was Mozart in the habit of writing useful musical ideas on scraps of paper? The inherent implication is that, at a later time and as a matter of common practice, he expanded on and incorporated music written on such scraps into his compositions.

But no matter how the statement is interpreted, the belief that such scraps of paper supplied Süssmayr with useful information makes no sense in the context of a Mozart composition. Mozart did not compose by creating diverse scraps that contained various musical fragments, which were then used as raw material for the creation of his manuscript scores. Not a single case is known in which Mozart composed in this way. Nor did he fashion ideas for future use in this manner. The only Mozart manuscripts that exist today in private collections and formal repositories that can be accurately referred to as "scraps" were invariably cut from larger sheets some indefinite period of time after Mozart died, sometimes for the purpose of enhancing sale prices.

So a literal approach to what Constanze is alleged to have said encounters a roadblock at once. Had the words "sketch," "draft," or even "paper" been used, her alleged statement might be considered helpful, but here no useful information is transmitted by Constanze's supposed remark about "scraps." In fact, it is worse than no information at all because it represents a condition so divorced from Mozart's normal practice that no reliable conclusions can be derived from it.

It would be hard to argue that in this one case Mozart took an unprecedented approach to composing; that is, by writing useful compositional information on scraps of paper that he intended to incorporate as part of the work's final content. To argue so is neither rational nor useful.

This forces us into the position of reinterpreting the statement. The only way that makes any sense is that Constanze gave Süssmayr some musical sketches, albeit of unknown content. But it turns out that this description, too, has problems of its own.

When Mozart sketched or drafted material, he generally did so on a leaf of paper (measuring approximately 12½ x 9 inches, or sometimes a little smaller, depending on what size paper was available to him). The sheet containing the Amen fugue sketch (see Illustration) is not atypical. A full sheet of paper slightly larger than our standard office stationery today would not normally be called a scrap. So, perhaps one of the difficulties that we have here is simply an over-specific translation of "Zettelchen."

Also, one must consider that any statement from Constanze about supplying Süssmayr with productive documentation in any form could have been exaggerated. Any assertion about the existence of sketches, drafts, or scraps would encourage the belief that the *Requiem* was entirely the work of her late husband. In fact, the more sketches she asserted to have existed, the stronger her case. Taken far enough, it makes the music she eventually delivered to Wallsegg unimpeachable; that is, she could claim that Süssmayr's work was derived entirely from Mozart's original thoughts as contained in the sketches she allegedly gave him.

Then there is the matter of her superficial knowledge of music. It is true that she sang, could play the piano, and read music, but these rudimentary skills are light years away from the technical sophistication needed to discern whether a particular sketch by her late husband was *Requiem*-related. Keep in mind the complex logic that the late Wolfgang Plath — one of the world's leading Mozart scholars — employed to deduce that he was examining a sketch of a fugue intended for *Requiem* use. The conclusions he reached about that sheet's music were anything but obvious.

It is impossible to accept that Constanze could have concluded such things considering her limited technical skills. Even if she had had several sheets of *Requiem* sketches, which is questionable to begin with, it is unlikely that she would have been able to understand their purpose, or determine whether they contained material destined for use in the *Requiem*. And then, we have Maximilian Stadler saying that she did not even know what the papers from her husband's desk were.

There is also the matter of how Mozart used sketches during composition. While there were cases in which he employed them, he did not do so as a matter of course and none of his mature compositions is known to have used them abundantly. Sometimes all the sketches needed for an entire work might appear on one side of a single leaf. Sketches came about when he was faced with a technical problem, one that he would begin to work out on a separate sheet of paper, as was the case with the *Amen* fugue that is one of only two known *Requiem* sketches found thus far (with both sketches on the same surface). Mozart, unlike Beethoven, for example, did not compose by sketching things out and then deriving his completed compositions from those sketches. The stories about the scraps require us to ignore this reality because it does not fit in with what we want. It would be uncharacteristic of Mozart to have generated many sketches for any single composition.

One contemporary specialist, Ulrich Konrad, has contributed enormously to scholarship devoted to Mozart's use of sketches as part of the creative process. He is perhaps the world's leading expert in Mozart's sketch material. In fact, the study of Mozart sketches and their role in his creative process is almost entirely Konrad's invention. In addition to writing about the ways in which Mozart employed sketches, Konrad's studies have documented the character and content of every known sketch. He was even instrumental in the publishing of a collection of facsimiles of Mozart's sketches. They number approximately 99 sheets of paper, 73 of which are written on both surfaces of the sheet and 26 of which are written on only one surface. As far as anyone can say, these 99 sheets constitute the entirety of what remains of Mozart's sketches.

Any surface may contain sketches from several different sections of a composition, or even sketches from several unrelated compositions. These 99 sheets contain approximately 320 distinct sketches. With respect to the sizes of these 99 pieces of paper, only two are less than eleven inches wide, the smallest (in writing area) being a slip eight inches by one-half inch, cut from a larger sheet. The second smallest is five and one-half by two and one-half inches, also cut from a larger sheet. There is a belief that Constanze may have destroyed some of her husband's sketches, namely those made for compositions that Mozart completed. She apparently thought them to be of less value than sketches made for unfinished works. When one examines the sketch repertoire compiled by Konrad, it becomes obvious how little material there is for each completed composition. Contrast the almost one hundred sheets with sketches on them (plus whatever Constanze might have destroyed), with approximately 430 drafts of incomplete compositions plus an uncertain number of complete compositions (with various estimates well above the generally accepted number of 626 works that Mozart is crediting with having composed), some with manuscripts of hundreds of pages. That contrast yields only a small percentage of sketches for each drafted or complete composition. Those sketches that exist are enormously important (and often fabulously valuable, as can be seen by auction prices), but on a sheet-quantity per composition basis, there are not many of them.

All this being taken into account, any assertion about material that may have been passed along in the form of scraps or sketches from the *Requiem* is difficult to sustain. It was only the identification of the *Amen* fugue sketch that brought about a resurgence in the belief that perhaps there were more such items.

All the credulity we bring to such notions, once again, reflects our desire to have the balance of the universe set right when we are faced with a situation that breaks our hearts.

TOO GOOD FOR SÜSSMAYR

The most common argument for rejecting Süssmayr's exclusive authorship of most of the *Lacrimosa* as well as the sections entitled *Sanctus/Osanna, Benedictus/Osanna*, and *Agnus Dei* speaks to the subjective issue of quality. It takes many guises but they can all be reduced to one argument: the sections in question are said to be too good to have been written by Süssmayr or, to put it another way, those sections are said to be so good that only Mozart could have written them. The well-known and respected conductor Nicholas Harnoncourt made a statement on this matter in an essay that appears in the program notes for his 1999 recording of the *Requiem*. He said,

> I cannot consider the [*Sanctus, Benedictus*, and *Agnus Dei*] as musical foreign bodies; they are essentially Mozartean. I find it misleading and impossible to believe that an inferior composer such as Süssmayr, whose works never rose above banal mediocrity, should have been able to write ... this *Sanctus, Benedictus*, and *Agnus Dei*... As far as I am concerned, they are also by Mozart... The obvious discrepancy of quality between the composition itself and Süssmayr's orchestration confirms me in this view.

Such quality-based assertions pass a superficial test of reason, are easy to state, and are effortless for a reader to accept uncritically; but they are both bankrupt and without substance. Furthermore, they are liable to objective criticism.

It is safe to say that the vast majority of those who use the "Too Good For Süssmayr" argument have never heard a single thing composed by the man, with the exception of the *Requiem* sections attributed to him. Little of his music is published, recordings of his works are rare, and one can easily spend a lifetime listening to and participating in music performance without coming across a single program in which his music has been played. This situation is changing, but ever so slowly. For example, in December 2003, the Romanian Mozart Society of Cluj-Napoca presented a nine-day series of music programs and technical conferences entitled "Mozart and Süssmayr." Present and participating was Dr. Erich Duda, perhaps the world's leading Süssmayr authority. His 1994 Viennese dissertation, *"The Musical Works of Franz Xaver Süssmayr,"* gives a table of the composer's compositions as well as a good deal of ancillary information about Süssmayr.

But despite Duda's significant efforts, it remains true that any assertions about Süssmayr's compositions, positive or negative, rarely have any objective basis. How could anyone know if Süssmayr were a sterling composer or a bad one? Most people know very little about him except for the irrelevant truth that he was not Mozart. Only a few specialized scholars are in any position to know the least thing about Süssmayr's creative abilities, much less to offer qualitative judgments about their merits.

During his lifetime, he achieved a position of respect. By 1799, he held the post of Imperial-Royal Kapellmeister, which attests to the fact that some influential contemporaries thought well of his music. He was not unprolific, having written multiple works in almost every form: masses, requiems, other church works, arrangements, stage works, ballets, operas, compositions that involved collaborative authorship, songs and miscellaneous vocal works, symphonies, sets of dances and marches, six concerti (including fragments and completions of the concerti of others), chamber music, piano compositions, and eighteen miscellaneous items, the *Requiem* completion being placed in that category. During his lifetime, Süssmayr's music was frequently performed. The reports from that era are generally positive, though he seems to have gone out of favor by 1800. Information about him is beginning to become more available, including on the Internet.

The temptation to reject out of hand any claim for Süssmayr as the composer of certain *Requiem* sections is based on a fallacy and on unsupported assumptions about the quality of his work. Almost no one is in a position to make judgments about Süssmayr's abilities as a composer; and furthermore, the suggestion that he was not a good enough composer would not be grounds for rejection even if his compositions were well known. There are three reasons for this.

First, judgments about his quality as a composer will never have a conclusion, since such judgments cannot be objective. Opinions on such things are often divided, and can change over time.

Second, there is no way to gauge how Süssmayr's level of creativity was affected by the task that he faced in completing the *Requiem*. Ordinary men sometimes do extraordinary things, given the right circumstances. Considering the situation, the challenge of completing Mozart's masterpiece could have brought him to a far higher plane of emotional intensity than any he had ever experienced.

Third, the assessments of his capabilities are biased simply because he was not Mozart. But then, who was? And with respect to this argument, a good deal more can be said.

Every music lover takes pride in a personal ability to treasure the good and reject the bad. But, on occasion, what is thought good or bad derives not from the content of a work, but who the composer is thought to have been. Nowhere was this shown more strongly than in the *Jena* symphony, a composition said to have been written by Beethoven. Notes on old 78 r.p.m. recordings suggested that the work portrayed Beethoven's intensity, his characteristic instrumental voicings, his nobility of spirit, his love of liberty and freedom, and so forth. But after musicologist H.C. Robbins Landon established that the work was by a man named Witt, it was performed far less frequently. Today, it is almost never heard.

Practically on signal, the words "trite," "threadbare," and "repetitious" began to be heard. This may have been driven more by the fact that few had ever heard of Witt than by the musical character of the *Jena* symphony.

In Mozart's case, that phenomenon has occurred a number of times. For example, a concerto of unknown authorship for multiple wind instruments called the *Symphonie Concertante* became all the rage when, in the latter part of the nineteenth century, it was offered as a newly-discovered composition by Mozart. Statements can be found suggesting that, despite the lack of documentary evidence in support of authenticity, the work had to be by Mozart because its quality was so distinctive. Then, its legitimacy came under attack with one critic suggesting that "the man who wrote that work could not compose." In 1964, it was officially removed from the body of Mozart's music when it was moved to a section of the Köchel catalog reserved for doubtful and spurious compositions. Once again, performances became less frequent, as some critics reversed their positions, despite the fact that the work, in part at least, may well be by Mozart!

There is a final inverse perspective to the "Too Good for Süssmayr" argument. It suggests that if Süssmayr were a good composer, more of his music would have survived the test of time and we would be more familiar with his works. But the idea that he could not have been a good composer because almost nothing by him is heard today begs the question of what would have become of Johann Sebastian Bach, had not Mendelssohn devoted such efforts on behalf of his legacy.

While it is certainly conceivable that the "too good for Süssmayr" argument is correct, no one can prove that it is. Under the emotional circumstances of Mozart's death, it is conceivable that Süssmayr could have risen above his particular level of creativity — which, again, has never been established, in any case. With a touch of irony, one could even argue that in his completion he wrote below his normal level of inventiveness so as to avoid producing something distinctive that would conflict with Mozart's musical style.

The arguments offered here are closely related and merit a summarization. First, it is argued that subjective views of quality should have no influence on questions of authenticity. Second, few people have heard anything of Süssmayr's music, so their comments as to his calibre are unfounded. Third, even if a great deal of Süssmayr's music were known, that would still not be grounds for questioning the authenticity of the *Requiem* sections attributed to him. Fourth, any assessment of Süssmayr's music contains a built-in bias by virtue of his being defined, for all practical purposes, as "not Mozart." And fifth, it is no argument to assert that if he were any good, we would be hearing a great deal more of his music.

Statements are often made to assert that one particular work is better than another. The joy of music lies in its ability to produce such feelings in people. We would not spend so much time listening to it if that were not the case. But those emotions are not useful tools that provide answers when questions of authenticity are raised.

TUNE DUPLICATION

What conclusions about intent can be reached when a melody, a melodic fragment, or some variation of a melody, is found in two separate compositions written by two different composers?

For example, Jacques Offenbach's opera, *The Tales of Hoffman*, duplicates a fragment of music sung by the character Leporello in Mozart's opera *Don Giovanni*. Was Offenbach's quotation deliberate or accidental? In this case, strong evidence shows that the melodic duplication has a specific objective and is not happenstance.

Musical and dramatic purposes are served by the quote. In Offenbach's opera, Hoffman's current *inamorata* is, at the moment the quotation is heard, singing in a performance of the Mozart opera next door to the scene being played out in *The Tales of Hoffman*. Offenbach chose to duplicate Leporello's melody for the purpose of creating an explicit dramatic and musical analogy. Specifically, the character Nicolaus, whose duty includes standing by while Hoffman pursues women in Offenbach's opera is a parallel to Leporello, whose duties include standing by while Don Giovanni pursues women in Mozart's opera. If some different tune were being quoted, a question might exist; but the intention behind this borrowing of Leporello's tune is quite clear and deliberate.

There are an unknown number of *deliberate* cases in which a melody from one composition is also found in a work of another composer. Even Mozart intentionally quoted other composers, making no effort to disguise the quotation. For example, in at least three cases in his opera *Don Giovanni*, the borrowing is so deliberate that the conceit becomes a part of the plot. And, on hearing of the death of J.C. Bach, Mozart paid homage to the man from whom he learned so much by including one of his melodies in the slow movement of a piano concerto.

Still, one can think that the number of all such *intentional* melodic duplications is not large; probably in the hundreds, not thousands. In fact, it is sufficiently rare that a discovery of such a thing invariably results in an automatic presumption of deliberate design. The suspicion that one composer is intentionally duplicating the melody of another is reinforced when the duplication goes beyond simple pitch similarity and takes rhythm into account as well.

The American vaudeville circuit had a popular act that centered on the phenomenon of a tune appearing in different compositions. Eventually the vaudevillian, named Sigmund Spaeth, became a radio personality using his clever routine, finding similar melodies in often wildly different compositions. For example, he compared the first four notes of the tune of "Yes, We Have No Bananas," with the opening melody of Handel's "Hallelujah Chorus" from *The Messiah*, suggesting, perhaps with tongue in cheek, that the author of "Bananas" deliberately derived his tune from Handel's music. The identical pitches and rhythms of the two tunes, coupled with the ludicrous difference in musical genres, created a comical effect, indeed. Yet it may be that almost any tonal work will contain motifs that can be found in another tonal composition, and that phenomenon renders most tune duplications both accidental and meaningless.

Arguments about the authorship of sections of the *Requiem* have been examined in independent studies by two of the world's leading Mozart scholars, Robert D. Levin and Christoph Wolff, both of Harvard University. Those arguments were significantly different from anything that had ever been previously suggested about Süssmayr's contributions to the *Requiem*, because they strove for (and perhaps achieved) objectivity, a welcome and helpful change from the usual circumstances.

What Levin and Wolff said was this: some melodies found in the sections of the *Requiem* attributed entirely to Mozart may also be found — though occasionally with slight differences due to changes of pitch or rhythm — in sections of the *Requiem* for which Süssmayr claimed full credit. Not only did Levin and Wolff state this to be the case, but they also gave examples in which exactly that phenomenon was unambiguously demonstrated.

But this needs some clarification. It was not that one or more major motifs from the Mozart sections were necessarily major motifs in the Süssmayr sections. In fact, the particular duplications given as examples were discovered only after intense study. So hidden were those melodic duplications that some had never been noticed before. In effect, one might listen to the Süssmayr sections many times and not be conscious of those thematic similarities until they were pointed out. Thus, the prominence of such a phenomenon was not the essence of the discovery, but rather the fact that it occurred at all. It manifested itself, for example, as a melody found in the *Requiem aeternam* that appeared later in the bass line of a Süssmayr-authored section of the *Requiem*.

The main consequence of the Harvard scholars' important, forceful, objective, and well-illustrated argument was this: since it is improbable that such melodic duplications are accidental, the likelihood of Süssmayr's total authorship of the sections for which he claimed full credit is lessened.

Various scenarios come to mind. Melodies or fragments of melodies from those *Requiem* sections that are known to be by Mozart could have appeared in sections alleged to be by Süssmayr either because Mozart had directed Süssmayr to do that, or because Süssmayr had access to original Mozartean material destined for the *Requiem* — from the "scraps of paper" or otherwise — and simply included such melodies without giving proper attribution. Whatever the case, the authority of Süssmayr's complete authorship of the sections in question was injured by the hypotheses of Levin and Wolff.

However, the basic premise of these two distinguished scholars also is open to debate. Must we consider the presence of such duplications as meaningful events, at all? At first blush, the concept of *accidental* melodic duplication being a common activity — which may be the case — sounds outrageously counterintuitive. Given a melody consisting of a note followed by, say, any of four or five others, each of which may assume many different pitches, the number of melodies that can be so constructed appears to be astronomical, thus making accidental duplication very unlikely. But, as it turns out, the occurrence is quite common.

The melodic fragments used by almost all composers of the period were a far smaller subset than the theoretically possible maximum. The complete set of *all* melodic fragments of any given length contains intervals infrequently encountered in music of this period. A study of Mozart's music, undertaken for the purpose of examining this phenomenon, suggests that over his entire compositional life he used only a small percentage of the possible aggregate of pitch combinations. Most composers of this era did likewise. So do most tonal composers everywhere, even today.

The nucleus of frequently-used melodic fragments being so much smaller than the theoretically possible maximum, *accidental* melodic duplication will occur more often than one might have thought.

Much of the tune duplication that exists between any two compositions is absolutely mindless and meaningless. This situation most frequently occurs when a melodic fragment contained in some inner voice of one composition happens accidentally to agree with the same fragment found in the inner voice of another. But occasionally, and by pure chance, a fragment that is important to the music of one composition happens to appear in a prominent voice of another. The rhythm may be altered and the context utterly different, but the sequence of pitches is such that a tune from one composition can be shown to appear in another. And that is the kind of accidental melodic duplication that is looked upon as being meaningful.

This perspective that accidental duplication of tunes is the norm and not the exception — can be demonstrated in the following way. Comparing any two tonal compositions by any two composers who ever lived will reveal substantial quantities of meaningless melodic duplication, that is, a randomly chosen sequence of four or five contiguous but differently pitched notes found in one composition has a high likelihood of being found in the other. There may also be a small amount of tune duplication that appears meaningful, though it almost certainly is not. And that examination could be in combinations as bizarre as a contrast of Bruckner's *Ninth Symphony* with Stephen Sondheim's *Into The Woods*, or any part of Lehar's *The Merry Widow* contrasted with any arbitrarily selected section of Bernstein's *Age of Anxiety* Symphony.

A case in which a certain melodic fragment appeared prominently in at least seven different compositions written over a period of at least 200 years was found and documented by a Dutch musicologist, the late Marius Flothuis. His observation was a wry one and he drew no conclusions about the similarity, but it is a demonstration of how few so to speak atomic melodic particles are used by tonal composers.

The phenomenon of tune duplications can be illustrated by analogy to cooking. Two chefs may start with the same basic ingredients, but one makes a pleasant dinner while the other creates a masterpiece.

Examples of discovered melodic similarities have resulted in some strong assertions. Such was the case when, in 1991, it was claimed that Elgar's secret *Enigma* theme was taken from Mozart's *Prague* Symphony. That was probably an accidental melodic similarity, but one that produced a glowing report of the "discovery" of Elgar's secret in *The New York Times* on November 7, 1991!

In effect, the presence of similar or identical thematic fragments in any two compositions cannot, except under the most remarkable circumstances, be used to establish any historical, musical, or psychological relationship between them.

THE LESSER TALENT

Despite the arguments of the previous sections in support of Süssmayr's entire authorship of the *Requiem*'s disputed sections, there are and probably always will be some who reject any such conclusion. They listen only to their hearts in this matter. And who is to say that they should do otherwise?

Yet, there is still one final question worthy of examination, one derived from an assumption with which almost any Mozart lover will concur, namely, that Mozart probably had more talent as a composer than Süssmayr. But can a lesser talent create a brilliant work of art? Absolutely! Many astonishing examples found in the history of diverse art forms demonstrate it. Consider, for example, the Dutch painter, Hans van Meegeren.

Following the conclusion of the Second World War, van Meegeren was arrested and charged with having sold a Dutch national treasure to the Nazi, Hermann Göring. Specifically, he was accused of selling a newly discovered masterpiece, "Christ at Emmaus," which was attributed to Vermeer. Such an act was considered treasonable.

Prior to the trial, Van Meegeren defended himself with the electrifying statement that the charges were false, because the painting was a forgery! Further, he asserted that it was he who had forged the work in 1936-37. When his declaration was challenged, he proceeded to paint another "Vermeer," this time under observation, and showed the art world exactly how he had deluded both Hermann Göring and it. The charges of selling a national treasure were dropped, though van Meegeren did spend one year in prison for forgery.

It is not the intention of this anecdote to suggest that van Meegeren was a lesser talent, though his original canvases rarely sold well. In fact, his journey into forgery began because he found it difficult to make a living from his own paintings. But that he was a talented forger is obvious. By examining the approbation of art historians who declared his many forgeries to be genuine Vermeers, one can come to only one conclusion: that it is very possible for a lesser talent to create a brilliant work of art.

The 83-year-old art historian Abraham Bredius, on seeing van Meegeren's "Christ at Emmaus" in 1937, wrote in the *Burlington Magazine*, the art bible of the time,

> It is a wonderful moment in the life of a lover of art when he finds himself suddenly confronted with a hitherto unknown painting by a great master, untouched, on the original canvas, and without any restoration, just as it left the painter's studio! And what a picture! ... [W]hat we have here is a ... masterpiece of Johannes Vermeer of Delft.

Furthermore, van Meegeren's "Christ at Emmaus" was not his only forgery, so it cannot be argued that his success was simply the result of luck. He painted and sold at least two works in the style of Pieter de Hooch ("The Card Players," and "The Drinking Party"), and a number of other works that were attributed to Johannes Vermeer, including "The Last Supper," "Isaac Blessing Jacob at Christ's Feet," and "The Adulteress." Even in the face of overwhelming proof of his forgeries, some art lovers believed in the authenticity of van Meegeren's "Vermeers" until the day they died.

Nor was Van Meegeren's success unique. The forger Elmyr de Hory sold many counterfeit paintings and sketches to galleries and museums; the story was first told in the book *Fake*, by Clifford

Irving. Oddly, Irving himself later forged a book that he asserted to be the autobiography of the American millionaire and eccentric, Howard Hughes, and both of these peculiar tales were made into a film by Orson Welles. As a participant in this chain of deception, Welles was the party who created the 1938 hoax that frightened large portions of America into panic by his realistic radio broadcast about Martians with poison gas invading New Jersey.

Leaving the world of painting, one finds a number of examples of literary forgeries or hoaxes in which an author successfully passed off self-authored works as the writings of another individual. Notable was the case of Magdalene King-Hall's *The Diary of a Young Lady of Fashion in the Year 1764-1765*, published by Meredith Press of New York in 1967. As a result of excellent reviews, it was an immediate sensation. Unfortunately, it turned out to be a fraud. Though not a genuine parallel to the Süssmayr/Mozart or Van Meegeren/Vermeer cases, it shows that frauds occasionally get by the eyes of experts.

Forgeries exist everywhere in art and related disciplines: furniture, antiques, archeological "finds" including Greek statuary and Mayan pottery, stamps, coins, jewelry, precious stones, and *objets d'art*. Even forged fine wines have been produced.

The world of Mozart's music is not immune to this phenomenon. A number of inauthentic compositions have been advertised — some successfully — as the creation of the Salzburg master. Inauthentic violin concerti and even some compositions alleged to be early symphonies have been considered part of the canon of Mozart's music at one time or another. Some of these compositions were outright forgeries created for the sole purpose of being passed off as genuine Mozart. Others may have been put forward with less criminal motives, for example when someone discovering a work by an unknown composer succumbs to the subconscious desire that it be authenticated as a work by Mozart. One such instance, a mass in G now relegated to the Köchel catalog's appendix for questionable compositions, insinuated itself into the Mozart repertoire as early as 1819 when it was published as genuine by the British firm of Novello. Republished in 1829 and again in 1850, the work was not attributed to its real author, Wenzel Müller, until 1972, the story being further complicated by the fact that two different composers, both contemporaries of Mozart, bore that same name.

There still remains some number of compositions published at this very moment bearing Mozart's name as composer though they are misrepresentations. Even the reverse has happened, namely a genuine Mozart composition (actually a cadenza for a piano concerto, though not in Mozart's hand), was declared "not by Mozart" on the basis of a reviewer's perspective. And then the original manuscript of that very cadenza, and in Mozart's own hand, was discovered in Latvia!

Almost the same scenario occurred with a Vermeer. An ironic twist on van Meegeren's forgeries resulted in at least one apparently genuine Vermeer to fall under a cloud of suspicion. Only in July 2004, did "Young Woman Seated at the Virginal," suspected of being a forgery because of the van Meegeren scandal, become vindicated when it was sold in Sotheby's London facilities for $30,000,000. The painting had languished in near obscurity following van Meegeren's disgrace. Even a description of the painting in a seventeenth-century sales catalog failed to lift the cloud of concern about its legitimacy. Fully ten years were spent in study and testing by a group of scholars, museum curators, painting conservators, costume authorities, paint analysts, and auction house experts until confidence in it validity was restored.

In its most elemental terms, Süssmayr took part in a forgery when he composed movements of the *Requiem* that were advertised as being by Mozart. It certainly was not for personal gain or fame that he took part in the effort, but that does not allow one to conclude that what he did was not forgery. Certainly, it was not on the grand scale of Van Meegeren's Vermeers, an effort undertaken entirely for personal gain. But make no mistake about it. Süssmayr's intent was to deceive.

Despite history's proof that works by lesser talents have been and continue to be accepted as the genuine efforts of acknowledged masters, some music lovers will probably always continue to believe that Süssmayr's work on the *Requiem* was guided by Mozart's hand, either personally or posthumously.

We are, after all, speaking about matters of the heart.

BRUSSELS DESECRATION

Having discussed the eight sections that Mozart finished architecturally but left deficient in instrumental detail, and the one that he left in a state that prevents a traditional completion, we have come to the end of the discussion about the portion of the autograph in Mozart's hand. We will go on to complete the story of the writing of the entire composition by speaking about the five additional sections added by Süssmayr, but before that, we must pause to tell one final detail — paradoxically, a contemporary one — that speaks of the manuscript's desecration in 1958. It is a tragic moment in the story of the original manuscript and addresses itself to the worst in people, or, to be more precise, the worst in one unknown, selfish, profaning thief.

In the section entitled "Second Dimension," we discussed the generally held, but almost certainly incorrect belief that the eighth measure of the *Lacrimosa*, was the last music that Mozart would ever write. While this cannot be proven, it makes much more sense to speak about a passage elsewhere in that same manuscript. Specifically, the last entry of Mozart's life was, in all likelihood, the writing of four words that occur at the end of the last page of the manuscript, the lower right hand corner, to be precise. The subject of this section is the tragic story about that small portion of the autograph and of its violation in the twentieth century.

Mozart chose to end the ninth and tenth sections (*Domine Jesu/Quam olim* and *Hostias/Quam olim*) of the *Requiem* with the same brief fugue, named *Quam Olim*. Rather than write out the same music twice, he wrote it once at the appropriate place in the *Domine Jesu* (which is why that section is referred to as *"Domine Jesu/Quam Olim"*), and then noted that it was to be repeated at the conclusion of the *Hostias* (which is why that section has been consistently referred to as *"Hostias/Quam Olim"*). That is a common shorthand technique used by composers for sections heard more than once in performance. The process of musical composition often includes abbreviations that call for certain sections to be repeated.

In this case, Mozart's directions take the form of four words. The text, written in Italian, at that time the standard Western language for music, reads, *"Quam olim, Da Capo,"* which means, "Begin a repetition of the entire *Quam olim* section at this point." The term *Da Capo* means, in this sense, "take it from the top," or "start over." At a much later time, these words and their placement in the manuscript at this juncture were given a touching emotional significance by the family friend and musician Maximilian Stadler, who wrote, "It is most remarkable that the last words [Mozart] wrote ... following the *'Hostias'* were *'Quam Olim, Da capo,'* as if he wished to denote that he himself was now passing into the eternal life promised by God to Abraham and his seed."

In 1958, by special arrangement with the Austrian National Library, the manuscript of the entire *Requiem* was placed on public display at the Brussels World's Fair. In an unguarded moment, a thief ripped out the portion of the page containing the words *"Quam Olim, Da capo."* It has not been seen since. Today, no one but that larcenist knows where it is. The perpetrator must have been familiar with the history of the *Requiem*, prizing those words that are believed to be the last thing written in Mozart's hand. Now, that profoundly symbolic relic has vanished from the public domain; as a stolen object, it can never openly be sold or displayed or even shared with scholars.

THE THIRD DIMENSION

The *Requiem*'s first dimension of impairment dealt with the eight architecturally complete but instrumentationally deficient sections. The second dimension dealt with the special case of the *Lacrimosa*, a section missing architecture and definition, deficiencies that combined to prevent the kind of a completion that was possible with the first eight. Now we come to the third dimension: even after the problems of the first and second dimensions were repaired, the *Requiem* was still liturgically unsuitable; the religious obligations of a mass for the dead were far from finished at the point where the *Hostias/Quam olim*, Mozart's final drafted section, was concluded. Music appropriate to the additional devotions had to be created.

Following the *Hostias/Quam olim*, Süssmayr chose to add five additional sections to give the entire composition greater breadth, scope, and duration. Of the five sections, the available evidence coupled with the lack of evidence to the contrary suggests that the first three were composed entirely by Süssmayr and without any substantive assistance from Mozart, though the controversy about that still goes on. The final two sections repeat the *Requiem aeternam* and *Kyrie* heard earlier, though the repeat is not exact. Besides beginning the penultimate section, *Lux aeterna*, in a major key, some rhythms are altered due to the syllabification of the changed text. Despite these differences, the final two sections remain a further but posthumous contribution from Mozart, though there is no reason to believe that, had he lived, he would have concluded the *Requiem* in this fashion.

It is possible that the first three sections added by Süssmayr were, conceptually, proposed or hinted at by Mozart. A dying man could have conveyed some idea of the three sections with a few short, pithy statements. However, the peculiarity of the inclusion of the final two sections of the *Requiem* is almost never spoken about in the literature. It is mentioned, of course, but invariably in a single brief statement that notes the presence of the two sections, most often without commentary. Perhaps writers want to close the matter out as quickly as possible — it is difficult and controversial enough to explain what happened up to that point. But the ending should not be dismissed so rapidly, because the origin of the final two sections is, itself, controversial. Specifically, the two key players, Constanze and Süssmayr, contradict each other concerning whose idea it was to conclude the *Requiem* in this way.

The first section added by Süssmayr consists of two parts. First, there is a brief introduction of ten measures in a slow tempo (*Sanctus*) that connects directly and without interruption to a short fugue (*Osanna*). At only 27 measures, the fugue is too short for the dramatic and musical purposes it needs to serve.

That this section uses the word "Osanna" may tell us something. On those musical occasions in which Mozart used this word, it is always spelled "Hosanna." While there is no fundamental linguistic or theological difference between the two words, there is a technical one. For the singers, "Osanna" begins with stopped breath and closed throat, while "Hosanna" begins with continuous breath and open throat. The choice of "Osanna" contradicts Mozart's consistent practice, and is therefore further evidence of Süssmayr's involvement — and Mozart's uninvolvement — with this section.

There are other ways in which Süssmayr specifically deviated, in this and the two sections of the *Requiem* that follow, from Mozart's lifelong compositional practices. This is not to suggest that Süssmayr was ignorant but only to show evidence of his and not Mozart's authorship, though this does not mean that the sections were not influenced by Mozart's hints. Even in the face of suggestions supplied by Mozart, the realizations by Süssmayr could well have been according to his own habits.

The *Sanctus/Osanna* is a case in point. It is written in a way that is explicitly and specifically uncharacteristic of Mozart, especially in the writing for wind instruments. The first anomaly is the key signature in which the basset horn pair is obliged to play. In the *Sanctus*, those instruments have a key signature that is unprecedented in Mozart's writing for members of the clarinet family. Nowhere in Mozart's work, and scarcely ever in the entire body of music up to 1800, are clarinets or basset horns written in a key that requires more than one sharp. Yet here, in the *Sanctus*, the key signature calls for three sharps, an act that violates Mozart's consistent and lifelong practice and the explicit directives of every treatise of the eighteenth century discussing the clarinet family and how to write for it.

This is followed by a second aberration that begins in the *Osanna* fugue. There, two bassoons duplicate the music of the tenor and bass voices of the chorus, whereas the basset horns are suddenly silenced for no comprehensible reason. And because they are silent, they do not support the soprano and alto voices as they do elsewhere and should have been doing here. In effect, this scoring is completely inconsistent with Mozart's practices and differs from the way in which these instruments are used in a repeat of this same music in the next section of the *Requiem*.

> *(Sanctus)*
> *Holy, holy, holy, Lord God of hosts,*
> *Heaven and earth are filled with your glory.*
>
> *(Osanna)*
> *Hosanna in the highest.*

The second section, the *Benedictus/Osanna*, also consists of two parts, the first of which connects directly with the second, as in the *Sanctus/Osanna*. The *Benedictus* is 53 measures long, while the recapitulation of the *Osanna* is 23 measures long, four measures shorter than its first presentation — compounding the error of it being too short in the first place.

While that reprise of the *Osanna* fugue superficially appears to be a repeat of the same music heard in the previous section, it is not. It has been re-engineered, shortened by four measures, and presented in a different instrumental dress. Here, strangely enough, Süssmayr uses the wind instruments quite differently. The two basset horns support the soprano and alto voices of the chorus, while the two bassoons support the tenor and bass voices — unlike what was done the first time around.

(Benedictus)
Blessed is he who comes in the name of the Lord.

(Osanna)
Hosanna in the highest.

One possible reason why Süssmayr may have chosen to rescore the *Osanna* fugue instead of simply duplicating the material he had already written earlier — as Mozart did for the twice-used *Quam Olim* fugue — could be that the second presentation of the *Osanna* is in a different key than the first one. This is considered to be a particularly severe technical blunder and it has been "corrected" in several more recent recompletions of the *Requiem*, which we will discuss later on. The second presentation of the Osanna fugue should, we presume, have been in the same D major key in which it was heard earlier. Whatever the reason for Süssmayr's choice of a different key signature, which led to the recomposition of the fugue, it is objectively uncharacteristic of Mozart.

Anomalies such as these preclude any possibility of Mozart's direct involvement. While he certainly could have given Süssmayr directions to include a *Sanctus/Osanna* or *Benedictus/Osanna*, these peculiarities show that if Mozart participated at all, he did not provide any level of detailed technical explanation, such as would be typical in an act of dictation to an amanuensis. That point does not have any bearing on the question of whether the sections in question are beautiful music. Such judgments are in the hands of the individual listener. But, objectively speaking, we are on solid technical grounds when we say that the sections are uncharacteristic of Mozart.

The third section, *Agnus Dei*, begins the preparations for the conclusion of the work. It is 51 measures long and will feed, without pause, into the final two sections of the *Requiem*. It also serves, or is supposed to serve, the added purpose of adjusting the key so that the transition to the next or penultimate section of the *Requiem* does not produce an obvious seam in the harmonic connection.

Lamb of God who takes away the sins of the world,
Grant them rest. Grant them eternal rest.

Lux aeterna, the 30-measure long penultimate or fourteenth section of the *Requiem*, is an altered version of the *Requiem aeternam* that opened the work thirteen sections earlier. The connection by which it is attached to its predecessor, the *Agnus Dei*, has to accomplish certain adjustments, which partly explain the differences between it and the *Requiem*'s first section on which it is based. This is followed immediately by the fifteenth section, the 52 measure *Cum sanctis* fugue, the final music of the *Requiem*, and which is based on the *Kyrie* fugue heard earlier.

(Lux aeterna)
Let everlasting light shine upon them,
in the company of your saints in eternity, Lord,
because you are merciful.
Lord, give them eternal rest,
and let everlasting light shine upon them.

(Cum sanctis tuis)
With your saints in eternity,
for you are merciful.

Constanze and Süssmayr give inconsistent accounts about whose idea it was to repeat the first two sections as music for the last two. Constanze, in a 1799 statement, asserts, "Mozart told [Süssmayr] that if he were to die before he finished it, the first fugue should be repeated at the end, which was customary, anyway." In this case, it sounds fairly credible in that it is the kind of brief instruction that a dying man could convey; however, Süssmayr contradicts her, and the statement's reliability is questionable for another reason as well.

A significant weakness in Constanze's assertion is found by her gratuitous comment that such a reprise "was customary." That is not at all clear. No formal rules require music for a mass, requiem or otherwise, to end as it began, though there were no formal rules against it, either. Perhaps her comment was an attempt to justify what is, in reality, another anomaly. Besides the *Requiem*, Mozart wrote sixteen complete masses (none of which is a requiem mass and all of which have a Salzburg tradition and were written years earlier). While some of these works do employ a brief recapitulation of the opening theme, in not a single one of these sixteen masses does the final section repeat the opening material to such a literal extent and degree as is found in the *Requiem*.

Süssmayr's statement, made in 1800, explicitly contradicts Constanze's account. He says, "in order to give greater unity to the work, I took the liberty of repeating the *Kyrie* fugue to the words *Cum Sanctis*." So Süssmayr takes full credit for the idea, while Constanze suggests that it was entirely Mozart's conception.

All things considered, it is difficult to conclude that Constanze's version of the story is accurate. It appears to be another one of her constant efforts to maximize Mozart's contribution while minimizing Süssmayr's. The question appears to be safe; no conclusive answer can ever be found, since what Mozart did in the sixteen non-requiem masses that he composed in his early years is no guarantee of what he might have done in the *Requiem*.

THE *Requiem* IS COMPLETED

Süssmayr's completion of the *Requiem* is the least detailed portion of the story surrounding the composition's history; simply put, not enough facts are known about this portion to enable much investigation. What is missing is, first, information about the mechanical manner in which Süssmayr created the material that eventually went to Count Wallsegg's agent in satisfaction of the commission; second, information as to what Wallsegg's agent was told about the state of the work at the time of Mozart's death; and third, by what date Süssmayr completed his work — although evidence points to a date between March 1 and July 1, 1792. However, hazardous as it is to speculate, it is still possible, given some bits and pieces of the Requiem's history and applying the rational principle of selecting the simplest solution when many are available, to reconstruct a probable sequence of events.

We begin with the assumption that Constanze made the entirety of Mozart's manuscript score available to Süssmayr. Most likely he took possession of the document, and worked at home; that is, he was not required to come to Constanze's residence while he was working on the completion to get additional pages of the autograph. To this we can elaborate to some extent on what little is known about what Süssmayr turned over to Constanze following his completion of the work.

The first and most important item he gave her is the document generally called the "score for delivery." This is the manuscript of the Requiem that Constanze gave to Wallsegg's agent, though how and when she did that, and the details of what might have transpired during that transfer of ownership, are unknown. Either Constanze met with him and presented the score personally, or arranged for the agent to get it through an intermediary.

This is, perhaps, one of the most important moments in the Requiem's history because Wallsegg's agent might have been given some useful information about the creation of the score. It is almost certain that the agent was not given any information that could suggest that someone else had actually completed the work. If Wallsegg ever figured out that what he had was partially a forgery, it was probably not through details given at the moment of transfer of ownership of the score for delivery. The agent might have been told that the work was entirely by Mozart, with excuses offered for the months of delay between Mozart's death and delivery of the score. Alternatively, it is possible that nothing was said about authorship at all, leaving the agent to the natural assumption that Mozart wrote all of it. Excuses for the delay would probably also have been offered in this eventuality, too.

In effect, this historic moment is a body of information about which we know almost nothing. Without knowing what, if any, information or clues were transmitted at this juncture, we have no real insight into Wallsegg's perception of the work at the time he received it. The only thing we can be sure of is that Constanze would have made certain that she received the balance that was pending. That moment of transfer and the collection of fees owed are both the nucleus and the high point of this story.

The contents and organization of the score for delivery are also important. The first eighteen surfaces or nine pages of Mozart's original manuscript (the last surface of which is blank), namely the *Requiem aeternam* and the *Kyrie*, were separated from that original manuscript and became the first eighteen surfaces of the score for delivery. Those pages are the only ones Wallsegg received that contained music in Mozart's own hand. The remainder of the score for delivery — from the *Dies irae*, the third section of the *Requiem*, to the *Cum sanctis* fugue, the fifteenth and final section — is entirely in Süssmayr's hand.

Wallsegg did not realize that his manuscript was in different handwritings for several reasons. Süssmayr was able to mimic Mozart's handwriting to a fair degree, though a real Mozart manuscript specialist knowing what to look for can see significant but subtle differences in content and page design almost at once. However, no one with such qualifications was alive at that time. And, the score was almost surely handed over for delivery to Wallsegg without any comment on how it was completed.

But there is another factor that would have persuaded Wallsegg even more strongly that Mozart wrote the entire composition, and this might well have been the most influential. At first blush, it seems that Mozart himself reached out from beyond the grave to support the false belief that the work was entirely by him, for what appears in the upper right-hand margin of the first page of the manuscript are the words "*di me* [by me], W. A. Mozart, 792, mp." Sadly, the handwriting, though similar to Mozart's, is almost certainly a forgery done by Süssmayr. This conclusion is reached by an examination of two other Mozart signatures known to have been written by Süssmayr, and the shape of the letter "M," which is different from all the many known examples of genuine Mozart signatures. Specifically, Mozart always began the letter "M" from the top of the letter, never from the bottom as is the case in the forged signature.

The cryptic "792" is shorthand for the year "1792." Of course,

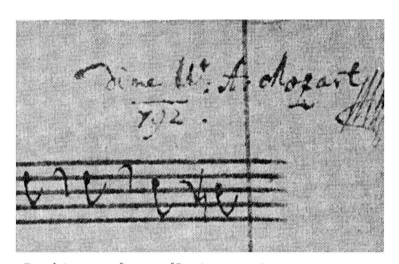

Forged signature on first page of Requiem manuscript.

Mozart was already dead by then. But can we dismiss it as his writing on that basis alone? Is it conceivable, by any stretch of the imagination, that Mozart could have post-dated a manuscript for a date in the future? A notebook of his compositions, begun in 1784, contains a projected end date written as "18__." So the idea that he could have envisioned completing the *Requiem* in 1792 and could have noted that date is not entirely out of the question. However, the signature is false, so that the credibility of everything in the upper right-hand margin of the page is damaged. The abbreviation "mp" is Latin for "*manu propria*," or "my own hand," shorthand that appears from time to time as part of Mozart's signature, though in this case it appears to be inauthentic.

However, with all these factors in place to encourage Wallsegg to believe in the deception that was being perpetrated, and with no handwriting analyst available to dispel any misconceptions, it is reasonable to assume that, when he received the score for delivery, Wallsegg did not know that Mozart had died without completing his commission.

The remainder of the score for delivery consists of 106 surfaces plus some blank surfaces and one additional leaf that contains, on one side only, trumpet parts for the Benedictus (in Süssmayr's hand, of course). Following the first eighteen surfaces of the score for delivery, the rest of it is entirely in Süssmayr's hand (and, as we shall see, was created in whole or in part in two distinct stages).

One can ask why Süssmayr did not use more of the original manuscript in Mozart's (and Eybler's) hand as part of the score for delivery. There are two probable reasons. Eybler's handwriting was quite different — one would not have to be a specialist to recognize the contrast, here — and Wallsegg and his intermediary would have spotted it immediately. The second reason is that Süssmayr had ideas of his own with respect to the completion, though he did incorporate some of Eybler's work as part of his effort.

Süssmayr eventually wrote out the rest of the score for delivery himself. However, some unknown part of that work was first done by drafting a working score. That working score, a second item that Süssmayr delivered to Constanze, is referenced in a letter from her, but its location, if it still exists — which is highly unlikely — is unknown.

The final step of Süssmayr's labor should have been to give Constanze the score for delivery, the remainder of the original manuscript (now reduced in size by eighteen surfaces), and his working score, along with anything else that he felt she might want or need. Then his task would be done. But it didn't happen that way.

Instead, he made at least one additional copy of his completion of the entire score for delivery, and possibly more. Some scholars suggest that he made a total of three additional scores, but no one is really certain. No matter how many copies he made, either then or later, there was a stupendous significance to his action. For reasons that will be expanded on shortly, the copy or copies that he made probably saved the *Requiem* from the unthinkable tragedy of eventual loss and destruction, the world knowing nothing of its existence.

Did he copy the score for completion of his own volition, or was it at Constanze's request? There is no record that Süssmayr kept a copy of the work for himself. It is extremely unlikely that he would have made copies of the score for delivery for anyone else, then, without being asked to do so.

ENDS AND MEANS

Sound of Thunder, a short story by science fiction writer Ray Bradbury, centers on how an insignificant event can have enormous historical consequences. In Bradbury's tale, the course of history is dramatically altered forever by a time-traveler who accidentally kills a butterfly, and the lesson could be a metaphor about what might well have been the *Requiem*'s fate.

Constanze's questionable behavior with respect to the details surrounding the *Requiem*'s completion occurred in a context that raises the frightening specter of a great loss to humanity. Had she taken a slightly different course, it is almost certain that the work would have been lost to the world forever. Here, we examine how a cultural catastrophe would have occurred had Constanze not done what she did.

Essentially, the facts are that Mozart was commissioned to write the *Requiem*, he died with the work incomplete, Constanze arranged for its completion, and Süssmayr did the work. Now, if we assume that it was Constanze's sole intention to satisfy the confidentiality conditions of the commission, collect the amount owed, and close out that sad section of her life, then when Süssmayr gave the score for delivery to Constanze, it would have been the only completed Requiem score in existence. Following this, Süssmayr would almost certainly have destroyed all of his source materials, including his working score and Mozart's original manuscript, except for the first eighteen surfaces that had become a part of the score for delivery. Constanze would have deemed this action necessary to prevent anyone from ever discovering that she had sold a partly forged work.

With the score for delivery now in her possession, Constanze would have contacted Wallsegg's agent, turned the material over to him, received the balance due, and put the matter behind her. Her tracks were covered; the fact that she had turned in a work falsely attributed to Mozart could never be proven.

Presumably, on receipt of the score, Wallsegg would have begun planning for a performance of the work in his wife's memory. He might even have had it performed annually for as long as he lived, or made arrangements for continued annual performances of the work following his death. It is unlikely that any of those performances would have taken place in or even near Vienna. He didn't live there — he sold his home in that city on December 19, 1791 — and visited it only on occasion as the needs of his gypsum business demanded. His performances of the *Requiem* would have taken place a considerable distance from Vienna and few Viennese would have had occasion to hear the work performed. Nor would anyone have sought it out, because, for reasons not yet explained, Mozart's name would not have been associated with any performance of the composition under Wallsegg's control!

So we envision performances of music for a requiem — with never a suggestion that it was partly an undocumented Mozart composition — given annually in the provincial area where Wallsegg lived. That would be Stuppach, 45 miles from Vienna, or, much more likely, in a larger town with the necessary resources in terms of space and musicians. That nearby large city would probably have been Wiener Neustadt, which, though only 21 miles from Vienna, is still far enough away to have attracted little notice. Even if it were performed in Vienna, there is little reason to suppose that anyone would have uncovered the secret of who had really composed the music.

If matters had followed that course, the musical world would never have known that Mozart had written or contributed to such a work. Eventually, memory of the music would fade, particularly as Wallsegg himself grew old. At Wallsegg's death, no one would have known anything about the music's real origin, and the composition would have played no role whatsoever in the core of the musical life of greater Austria.

The most fatal blow to the continued existence of the score for delivery occurs on the realization that Mozart was not the only composer from whom Wallsegg had commissioned music, and that Wallsegg's entire manuscript collection was eventually dispersed following his death. While the handsome, leather bound books from his private library (including some printed music scores) still exist in private collections, today only three of his secret commissions are known to have survived. One is a string quartet of unknown authorship held in a private collection, while the other two are works for flute (by Devienne and Hoffmeister) held in the archives of Vienna's Gesellschaft der Musikfreunde. The location and quantity of the manuscripts for the rest of his commissioned works are unknown, and it is most likely that they have all been lost or destroyed over time. Scholarly and musical interest in these few remnants is considerably heightened only because of Wallsegg's role in the commissioning of the Mozart *Requiem*. Without that connection, no matter how pleasant the music might be, hardly anyone would have been interested in the music library of an unknown and minor nobleman who happened to live in Stuppach, making his living in the gypsum business.

Add to the imagined scenario the certainty that there would have been no search for a lost *Requiem* by Mozart since no one, except Wallsegg, Mozart, Constanze, Eybler, Süssmayr, and Wallsegg's intermediary would have known of the commission, and none of these people would have had reason to gossip about it. At best, perhaps, some biographical material related to Mozart might include a curious remark to the effect that an unknown *Requiem* mass was rumored to have been written by Mozart on commission, but that no evidence of it had ever been found. The suggestion that he wrote a *Requiem* would be based entirely on unsubstantiated testimony including a statement of questionable reliability from Benedikt Schack, who sang the role of Tamino in *The Magic Flute*'s original production. Schack is reported to have said that he took part in singing a portion of the alleged work just eleven hours before Mozart died. But Schack's assertion cannot be corroborated. Since no reference to such a work appears in a personal catalog that Mozart created of his musical compositions, nor is there any mention of it in his correspondence, the notion would have to be dismissed.

It is Constanze who saved us from this sad eventuality. By her actions, unethical and probably illegal, she preserved the work for posterity. Her dealings were motivated by her need for money to feed her children; it is doubtful that her prime incentive derived from an appreciation of the magic that her husband had inserted into the *Requiem*. Exactly what did she do?

To begin with, after she settled accounts with Wallsegg through his intermediary, she made — or had made, over time — a number of additional copies of the *Requiem*'s score. She arranged for the work to have its first public performance even before Wallsegg was able to do it. After collecting her fee from the man who commissioned the work, she sold a copy of the score to the music-loving King Friedrich Wilhelm II of Prussia. (Shortly after Mozart's death, the king had requested scores for eight of Mozart's works from her and she complied, receiving a satisfactory price for them.) In early 1792, even before Süssmayr's work was finished, she agreed to supply this royal patron with a copy of the completed *Requiem* score. Her fee was exactly the price that Wallsegg had paid for his commission. Further, she claimed to have given two or three other copies to royalty and her defense of that action was the absurd assertion that when the manuscript was delivered to the party who commissioned it, she had reserved the right "to give copies to princes who, of course, would not publish them." Furthermore, her false stories about the work's history — given to many people, including biographers, to disguise the fact that the work was not composed by her late husband alone — were partly instrumental in contributing to the continuing unresolvable complexities about the *Requiem*'s history.

In Leipzig, she had two additional copies made in 1796, one of which was used for the first performance outside of Vienna (discounting two performances produced by Wallsegg in Wiener Neustadt, to be discussed shortly). The other was made for unknown purposes. The music publisher Breitkopf & Härtel later used one of these as the source for the first published edition. And shortly after that she provided a different music publisher, the firm of Johann Anton André of Offenbach, with a copy, which André used some years later to publish a second and competing edition.

Maximilian Stadler remembered that, before the work even appeared in print, "more and more copies were made and frequently circulated in Prague, Dresden, Leipzig, and elsewhere." In fact, so many copies of the score were surfacing that Breitkopf & Härtel had to assure themselves that their source for the first published edition was accurate.

Could Constanze have set off this chain of events in all innocence? A letter from her to Breitkopf & Härtel, dated May 25, 1799, on the eve of the first edition's appearance, shows that she was knowledgeable about the restrictions under which she should have been working. Constanze wrote, "I myself have never made [the *Requiem*] public, out of respect for the man who commissioned it *and who made nonpublication a condition* [italics mine]." Because the actual confidentiality agreement has never been found, its details are not known. But such a document would almost certainly have taken steps to prevent a good deal more than publication. Mozart's involvement would have been kept secret, performances of the work would have been forbidden, and a discussion of any details of the commission would have been impermissible.

As for Constanze "never [having] made [the *Requiem*] public," the duplicity of her comment is demonstrated by the fact that she arranged for the work's first public performance on January 2, 1793. It took place in a facility owned by one Ignaz Jahn, where many Viennese concerts were given. The profits she received from that performance are estimated to have been between three and four times the amount paid for the commission of the *Requiem* itself.

Süssmayr, who is alleged to have been in the audience at that first performance, received neither credit for his contribution nor any portion of the income Constanze gained from the performance. While today one can admire her entrepreneurial talent in recycling this one product and selling it in so many forms, Süssmayr had every right to resent being cut out of the process. These circumstances led to an alienation of their friendship and there is little evidence of any communication between them from that point to the date of Süssmayr's death in 1803 (of tuberculosis, aggravated by chronic alcoholism).

While we cannot be sure that Wallsegg was aware of that first performance, his subsequent behavior makes it seem likely that he was. Since he received the manuscript in the middle of 1792, it was probably his intention to have the work performed in his wife's memory on the upcoming anniversary of her death, February 14, 1793. But that date turned out to be only a few weeks after Constanze's first performance of the work, and rather than face a possible comparison from someone who might have been present at both events, he pushed the schedule for his commemorative event to the end of the year. Thus, it was not until December 14, 1793 that the work was performed for the purpose for which it had been commissioned, in memory of Countess Wallsegg. Following that, Wallsegg mounted one final performance on February 14, 1794 — the third anniversary of his wife's death — and then never again undertook to perform it.

However, when, towards the end of the century, Wallsegg learned of the forthcoming appearance of the first printed edition of the *Requiem*, he decided that this kind of contract violation could not be permitted. His attorney was directed to bring suit against Constanze, but even here his ace was trumped. She coyly indicated her willingness to supply Breitkopf & Härtel with the name of the man who had commissioned the work, making sure that Wallsegg was aware that his involvement would be made public. The publisher would, of course, have contacted Wallsegg in the same way they contacted Süssmayr; that is, to find out what his role was.

With that clever ploy, Constanze effectively checkmated Wallsegg. As we shall see, he had good reason not to want any publicity about his involvement. He could only accept Constanze's lame explanation that the published edition was prepared without either her knowledge or her consent, a statement that was patently false. At that point he dropped the suit and, while still retaining his anonymity, accepted a number of copies of the published score in compensation for his loss. He may also have received some small financial reimbursement.

Constanze had brilliantly, if shabbily, outmaneuvered him. The *Requiem* was now public, and would never be lost to the world.

COUNT WALLSEGG'S STORY

Wallsegg's wish to remain anonymous in this entire affair has been mentioned several times now; the reader may have come to the conclusion that his motivation for secrecy was derived from something monumental or heroic, perhaps a state secret that he was trying to protect. But his sad story does not end with a bang of revelation. Instead, it collapses with an embarrassing whimper. Wallsegg was, in terms of a polite euphemism, a *poseur*, a person who needed to impress others by making claim to a talent that he did not have. Specifically, he wanted to be seen by others as a gifted composer.

In order to satisfy his need to have a musical reputation for himself, he commissioned works from professionals and then put them forward as his own creations.

Until his commission of the *Requiem* from Mozart, he had bought from other composers mostly small stuff, perhaps impressive in quality but not requiring large instrumental and vocal resources: string quartets, piano trios, quartets for flute and strings, and other small chamber combinations. When the score of his secret purchase arrived from the commissioned composer, he would copy the original in his own hand, and then have performance parts copied out from that second score by the first violinist of his resident string quartet, Johann Bernard. No one besides Wallsegg, not even Bernard, was ever permitted to see the original manuscripts. Another composer who is known to have created works for Wallsegg anonymously was Franz Anton Hoffmeister, who happened to be one of Mozart's publishers. Hoffmeister is thought to have written a number of quartets for flute and strings for Wallsegg, though, like Mozart, Hoffmeister was probably unaware of his patron's identity. The musicians who played these works probably had suspicions about this eccentricity, but said little about it.

In three-hour afternoon music sessions held on Tuesdays and Thursdays at Stuppach Castle, music would be performed, and compositions falsely identifying Wallsegg as the composer were occasionally included. The Count was one of the performing musicians, playing either flute or cello. Those who suspected him probably thought this was a slightly pathetic but largely harmless self-indulgence for a man with money to spend.

However, when his twenty-year-old wife passed away, her death, coupled with his wish to be seen as a talented composer, caused him to take a larger step, and that is how we come to have the Mozart *Requiem*. The idea of having music for a requiem that promoted him as author, coupled with a desire to use that music to memorialize his youthful wife, was so compelling that he forged ahead without a full realization of the potential logistical and social complexities. By the time that Constanze got done with him a few years later, he probably regretted his action. But, who could have guessed that the selected composer would die with the work unfinished and thus ultimately expose his deceit?

Eventually, Wallsegg did come to possess a large-scale composition. However, this meant he would have to deal with music for an orchestra of multiple instrumental lines, some of which, the strings for example, required many players. A chorus and four vocal soloists were needed. This was performance on a considerably larger scale than what he'd been staging with his string quartet on Tuesdays and Thursdays. This fantasy was starting to look expensive, and, though he was wealthy, his resources were not limitless. Further, the costs of mounting performances of the *Requiem* came on top of the cost of the original commission of the work itself, plus those spent for his wife's tomb.

When his agent notified him that the score of the *Requiem*, commissioned approximately a year earlier, was now available — though its delivery, well past the first anniversary of his wife's death, was obviously later than requested — he took the first of many steps that would eventually land him in hot water. His first and most serious mistake came with the copying of the score for delivery. The original manuscript was partly in Mozart's handwriting but mostly in Süssmayr's, and he had to copy it in order to have a full orchestral score in his handwriting alone. That secondary score would be given to his music copyist. But he made an irreversible mistake. On the first page of his copy, he inscribed the words, "Composed by Count Wallsegg."

If he had not written this, he might have been able to talk his way out of any potential embarrassment at a later time. He could say, for example, "Of course, the work is by Mozart. I paid him handsomely for it, too, but I did not want his famous name and reputation overshadowing the memorial tribute to my wife. Instead, I wanted her soul to be the center of attention. This is why I requested that his name not be used." With such a story — as disingenuous and transparent as it is — and a willingness on the part of the listeners to turn both a blind eye and a deaf ear, he could have come out a hero. Instead, he ended up the goat.

It was Wallsegg's name as author, particularly after Constanze arranged for the first performance of the work as Mozart's composition at the beginning of 1793, that painted him into a corner. The score for delivery displayed Mozart's name as the composer (forged by Süssmayr, of course), and the score that he prepared from it had his name as the composer. Any publicity that might ensue could have resulted in requests to examine his score, and that would have destroyed his social position, his reputation, and possibly his business interests, too.

Thus, his behavior became very defensive. He dropped his suit against Constanze in 1799 at the first suggestion that she might release Wallsegg's name to Breitkopf & Härtel. His delay of an intended performance in early 1793, and his decision to perform the work only once more after conducting it as his own composition on December 14, 1793, were also consequences of his fear that the secret would get out. As a result of his withdrawal from the scene, when he died in 1827, no one realized that he owned the score for delivery of the Mozart *Requiem*, or at least no one knew where it was, or had found it. Only in 1838, some eleven years later, did its location and identity become known, and that was by accident. And as a final indignity, the *Requiem* itself, which had been or would be performed in ceremonies commemorating the death of Wallsegg's wife, as well as those of Haydn, Beethoven, Constanze, and both of Mozart's sons, was not performed at Wallsegg's death. No one thought of it. How ironic that the man who was inspired to commission this timeless composition — however mixed his motives may have been — would not have the music he had commissioned played at his own death.

There is a local Stuppach tradition that Wallsegg's score — the score for delivery, not the one he prepared as a copy of it — was actually found in 1838 in the house of the Stuppach Castle gardener, though how it might have gotten there is unknown. On Wallsegg's death in 1827, his sister became the sole inheritor of his estate, though her husband stepped in, took charge, and sold everything. Wallsegg's music collection went to a certain Joseph Leitner.

Now, the story, already murky with unsatisfactory details about the list of characters whose place in the *Requiem*'s history is uncertain, events that are obscure and unspecific, and a collection of *Requiem* scores that requires constant clarification as to which one is being spoken of, gets positively opaque.

Somehow the *Requiem* score for delivery passed from the hands of Leitner to a Stuppach musician named Karl Haag. He was a member of the orchestra that was used for Wallsegg's two performances of the *Requiem* and had developed a strong affection for the work, now forty-five years old. But, by 1838 Haag was dead, and ownership of his estate, which included the score for delivery, passed to a certain Katharina Adelpoller, widow of Wallsegg's usher at Castle Stuppach. Except for three minor works, there is no knowledge about what became of the rest of the music commissioned by Wallsegg and falsely claimed as his own compositions.

What happened next with the score for delivery will be covered in a later section. But a side issue derives from the manuscript's rediscovery. The manuscript of the *Requiem* was not discovered by someone who was looking for it, but was found by accident. The man who finally discovered the score for delivery was another former employee of Wallsegg who lived in Schottwien, the small village close to Stuppach where, in the local parish church, the remains of both Wallsegg and his wife now lay entombed. His name was Nowack (ironically the same name as the man responsible for the edition of the *Requiem* in Bärenreiter's publication of Mozart's complete works, 1956-1991) and in a less complicated story, his place would belong at the beginning of the tale of the *Requiem*'s rediscovery, not at the end.

It seems that Nowack had been asked to search for six unknown and unidentified Mozart string quartets. In that context, he was investigating the details of the disposition of Wallsegg's estate. How suspicion arose about the possible existence of the unknown string quartets is unclear, but a certain Count Moritz von Dietrichstein, an official at what is today the Austrian National Library, concluded that Wallsegg might have been the owner of those six unknown Mozart string quartets. Dietrichstein commissioned Nowack to investigate.

In Nowack's report to Dietrichstein on his search for the unknown string quartets — which probably never existed — he mentions his accidental discovery of the *Requiem*'s score for delivery. Actually, he thought that what he had found was the original *Requiem* manuscript entirely in Mozart's hand. He was wrong, of course, but that is what he, as well as everyone else, believed for some time.

Nowack spoke about a portion of the *Requiem*'s history, because it shed some light on the matter of the string quartets. He mentioned the lawsuit brought by Wallsegg against Constanze, whom he described as contritely asking Wallsegg "to consider her difficult circumstances and her poverty." Nowack then continues with his shocker, saying, "In view of this, *Count Wallsegg accepted six previously unknown quartets and other compositions that the widow offered him by way of compensation.*" [Italics mine]

Considering Constanze's adamant grip on her husband's compositions, as her only potential source of revenue, it is hard to imagine she would have parted with anything in order to buy off Wallsegg. There are other problems with the story, too. Nowack speaks of the lawsuit as having occurred because Constanze supplied a copy of the score "to a German publisher in Offenbach," implying an entirely different publisher than the one to whom Constanze supplied the copy.

But that is the kind of confusion that ensues when dealing with hearsay and second hand sources. Most of the main characters in the tale, the ones with the greatest knowledge of what happened, were all dead by the time Nowack was looking for the string quartets. It is a confused and mixed-up story, though as the prize for a scavenger hunt it contains a diamond at its center.

Count Wallsegg's legacy will make one final appearance when we get to the reassembly of the 80 surfaces written at least in part by Mozart in 1791. Wallsegg played his little conceited game in a provincial town, was immortalized because of it, and personally but indirectly provided the world with one of its most blindingly beautiful but flawed masterpieces — not unlike the Venus di Milo in that way — and never really received much pleasure from the whole thing. He lies today in a sealed vault in the parish church at Schottwien, off the beaten track and rarely visited by any who are grateful for what he provided. There are many tragic tales in the history of the *Requiem* but his, perhaps, is the most melancholy.

At the time of his death in 1827, Count Wallsegg's sister,

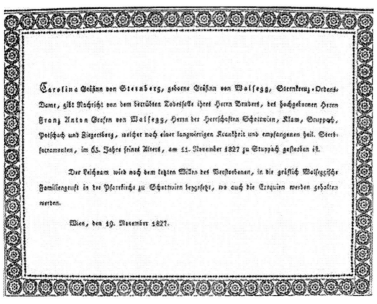

Count Wallsegg's death notice

Carolina von Sternberg, issued this death notice. Servants distributed these cards by hand to a select group of people, partly because the mail was too slow and the dead were buried quickly.

Such cards are still used in Austria today as death announcements. The text reads:

> Caroline Countess von Sternberg, born Countess von Walsegg [*sic*], member of the Sternkruez Order, announces the sad news of the death of her brother, the high-born gentleman Franz Anton Count von Walsegg [*sic*], lord of the domains Schottwien, Klam, Stuppach, Potschach, and Siegerberg. He received the last rites and died in the sixty-fifth year of his life on November 11, 1827 in Stuppach after having endured a long illness. In accordance with the last wish of the departed, the body will be buried in the Walsegg [*sic*] family tomb where the requiems will also be held.
> Vienna, 19 November 1827

SCANDAL!

The placement of this section is peculiar; it describes events that began before Wallsegg's death but continued after he passed away. And while there is no evidence that he was involved, it is difficult to believe that he was unaware of the notoriety that spread from the scandal. The central issue was a public and advertised assertion that the work called the Mozart *Requiem* was a fraud. Wallsegg must have viewed the controversy with mixed emotions, asking himself if he had been completely duped.

Many of today's music lovers want to — or even do — believe that everything in the work is, in one way or another, Mozart's creation. But in the era that we are about to examine, a segment of those who enjoyed music no less than we today were brought to hold the view that nothing in the work was by Mozart.

It began in 1825 with the publication of a polemical article entitled, "On the Authenticity of the Mozart Requiem," and, given the circumstances, there was almost no way to avoid the explosion of a public scandal. Constanze had so hidden and/or falsified the facts about the *Requiem* that stories of its origin became more and more convoluted, complicated, and contradictory. Eventually, the contorted tale that was going around strained the public's credulity to the breaking point. Constanze's web of deceit had finally ensnared her.

A German, Jacob Gottfried Weber, wrote the polemic. He suggested that not one note of the *Requiem* was Mozart's and that a fraud had been perpetrated on the public. While he did not say so explicitly, the only person who could have created the environment for such an accusation was Constanze, since she was the source of almost every assertion about the work's history and circumstances.

The specifics of Weber's occasionally bizarre analyses and proposals have been completely discredited, but the man was not a fool, nor was he musically illiterate. On the contrary, he was a composer and theorist of considerable influence with a particular interest in religious music. In 1814, he wrote a *Te Deum*, in 1816 music for a requiem, and shortly after that three non-requiem masses. He played the flute, piano, organ, and cello, invented a device that seriously challenged Maelzel's metronome, and was responsible for a precursor of the Wagner tuba.

Weber was also a successful attorney practicing law in Darmstadt (where he eventually became the General State Prosecutor) at the time he published the article. It appeared in a magazine named *Caecilia*, which was advertised as "A journal for the music-loving public, edited by a consortium of scholars, connoisseurs of the arts, and artists." *Caecilia* was in fact a one-man show managed by Weber as a vehicle for his opinions and comments on music topics. His *Requiem* inquiry had merit not because it was true but because it was an effort to expose the multiple contradictions about the work and its origins that had arisen over the years. Unfortunately, his method was less than rigorous, and consisted of little more than a series of casual opinions and hypothetical scenarios.

Almost 35 years had passed since Mozart's death. The *Requiem* had become an enormously popular work by 1825, because of the many performances made possible by the existence of a published edition of the full orchestral score. A vocal score was available as well as a complete set of orchestral parts. Yet not one of these publications — issued at different times between 1800 and 1812 — alluded to the fact that the work was not entirely executed by Mozart.

The publishers of the orchestral score, issued in 1800 by the firm of Breitkopf & Härtel — a powerful force in music publishing even today — did write to Süssmayr before publication to inquire about his role in the creation of the work's final form. They did so because, for the first time, Constanze had admitted his involvement, and very begrudgingly, at that. In a frank letter to Breitkopf & Härtel, written in February 1800 and made public in 1801, Süssmayr, for the first and only time in his life, made a statement about what he had done. There is no known reason to believe that anything he said was false or self-serving. His comments were revealing because his contribution had never been formally and publicly acknowledged by anyone, nor had he been given any credit or even mention in the then-published biographies of Mozart. Yet, despite the fact that his response reached Breitkopf & Härtel before their full score was released, they made no mention of Süssmayr's contribution. Nor was there any reference to him in the published vocal score or the orchestral performance parts. It is quite possible that no one at Breitkopf & Härtel — and few, if any, members of the general public — believed what he said. His remarks were not found credible, especially since they contradicted those of Constanze, the presumed authority on all factual *Requiem* matters.

Süssmayr's statement was the first time anyone with such inside information had ever publicly addressed the inevitable question of exactly what state the *Requiem* had been in at the time of Mozart's death. The question was only made more compelling by the contradictory information given by Constanze over the years, all of which was published under the assumption that its source was a guarantee of accuracy.

As one example of the *Requiem* contradictions that were current at that time, a published biography of Mozart stated that not only was the *Requiem* incomplete at the time of Mozart's death, but that the party who commissioned it received it in that incomplete form. Another said that Mozart completed the *Requiem* in its entirety prior to his death. Both biographers claimed that Mozart's widow provided testimony to these "facts." Such contradictions caused considerable confusion and Weber was determined to settle the matter. The idea was a good one, but unfortunately, his analyses were weak and his self-righteous and bombastic opinions on musical quality undermine the effort.

Weber stated that the score of the *Requiem* published by Breitkopf & Härtel in 1800 "[was] so incomplete that it can hardly be counted among [Mozart's] genuine works." He also volunteered to say that "It would distress me ... to believe, for example, that [in the *Kyrie*] it was Mozart who inflicted such warblings ... upon the chorus."

Weber invented a wildly complex and improbable scenario in which Mozart wrote not one, but two *Requiems*. Süssmayr finished one of them, based on an early collection of ideas that were barely fleshed out, and it was *this* dreadful piece that was being inflicted on the public as if Mozart had composed it. Weber stated that "the great Mozart would turn over in his grave upon hearing how his profound ideas have been debased by ... sounds that everyone assumes to have been written by him." (Never mind that he now calls "profound" those ideas that a moment ago were "barely fleshed-out.")

As for the second *Requiem* — in Weber's mind, the real one — he suggested that it disappeared entirely when it was given to the unnamed and still unknown patron who commissioned it and "has not — or at least not yet — seen the light of day." Wallsegg, if he read this material, would have known it to be false since he was fully aware that the manuscript he owned (i.e., the score for delivery) and the work published as the Mozart *Requiem* — the one being criticized by Weber — were one and the same.

Weber's bizarre theories inspired Beethoven, who read the article in *Caecilia*, to scrawl in its margin, "O you arch-jackass... O you double jackass." But not every expert dismissed Weber's ideas as irresponsible ravings; a composer as musically sophisticated as Robert Schumann agreed with him and thought of the *Requiem* as "not merely corrupt but wholly inauthentic except for a few numbers."

The entire affair finally blew over, and Constanze somehow came out of the situation not badly damaged. This is mostly because the now 68-year-old Maximilian Stadler came to the rescue by publishing a defense of the *Requiem*'s authenticity that smashed Weber's ill-conceived approach and his dull-witted arguments. Stadler's was a thoughtful and convincing document, but it repeated some old errors and introduced a few new ones, such as his gratuitous and exaggerated suggestion that the *Requiem* owed some of its melodic material to borrowings made by Mozart. It seems that every time one of the parties to the events surrounding the *Requiem*'s history made a statement that could clear up misconceptions, they also supplied further misleading and occasionally incorrect information that only complicated our understanding of the work's history.

In the end, it must also be admitted that Weber's periodical was losing subscribers and he may have been motivated in his writing as much by a desire to stir controversy and drum up readership support as by a scholarly desire to address the question of the *Requiem*'s origin. Perhaps the reading public did not like his attacks on Beethoven, Meyerbeer, and others, found in earlier issues of *Caecilia*. The magazine's publishers, Schott in Mainz, were putting pressure on him to boost the circulation. And then, too, jealousy may have played a part. Weber's son, Max von Weber, wrote a biography of his father in which he states Weber's belief that his own requiem was superior to Mozart's. Perhaps by criticizing the competition, he could at least improve his own position.

THE MANUSCRIPT IS REASSEMBLED

This section speaks of the remarkable circumstances surrounding the reassembly of the 80 surfaces of the entire *Requiem* manuscript. Of course, the contents of that manuscript had been altered following Mozart's death, mostly by the additions of Eybler, and this means that the reassembly did not recreate the document as it existed at the moment of Mozart's death. Today, that manuscript resides in one of the world's great repositories, the Austrian National Library in Vienna (which was the Imperial Court Library, at the time of the events discussed here). And while the value of the music is up to each listener to appreciate, the value of the manuscript can, in a certain sense, be estimated on the basis of the market.

There are several different ways of looking at Mozart's manuscripts. Music lovers think of them almost as holy relics, invaluable by any measure. Scholars view them in that way too, principally because they are objects worthy of serious study that hold secrets that enable one to understand a few things about Mozart's creative process. For sheer prestige, they are unbeatable. (The former owner of the entire manuscript of *Don Giovanni*, Pauline Viardot, would show it to specially invited guests. Liszt, Rossini, Gounod, Saint-Saëns, and others who were in awe of the opera would come to admire it. Prior to her death in 1910, she bequeathed it to the *Conservatoire de Paris*. In 1964, the Conservatoire combined its collections with those of the *Bibliotheque Nationale*, where the manuscript resides today.)

But another perspective, the financial, plays with the temptation to set a price on the "invaluable," and indeed such precious artifacts are a far more secure investment than real estate, stocks, or bonds. For their weight, they are more valuable than gold and diamonds. Because the autograph of the *Requiem* is an Austrian national treasure, the library would no more consider selling it than the government of the United States would sell the original of the Declaration of Independence. But if by some quirk of fate the original *Requiem* autograph were to be put up for sale, it is interesting to speculate what price the document might fetch at public auction. Manuscripts of Mozart's completed compositions are offered for sale so rarely that there is no real basis for comparison by which to project its commercial value. Nothing of the incredible history and emotional pull of the *Requiem* has ever come up for sale. Perhaps, since it is an incomplete composition, we should first examine comparables from the world of fragments to establish a profile and a possible theoretical sales price.

One Mozart fragment was sold, however, on June 6, 2001 at Christies' London auction house: a draft composition of only eight surfaces, two of which were blank. The work was an unfinished movement — exactly 161 measures from the start to the break-off point — for two pianos. Mozart abandoned it when he decided to use the same musical material in a composition for one piano, four hands.

We might use the worth of the unfinished two-piano manuscript as a benchmark in establishing a theoretical sale price for the *Requiem* autograph. This was not the first time that this fragment had seen the inside of an auction house. Christies' competitor, Sothebys, sold it to a Japanese businessman for £40,000 in 1989. That owner apparently thought it was time to cash in, and for the 2001 auction, Christies' manuscript experts estimated a sale price of between £50,000 and £70,000 (which would have meant a minimum profit of 25 percent, nothing extravagant for an investment of twelve years).

But when the all the bids were in and the hammer went down, the sale price, excluding commissions, had rocketed to £320,000 or $445,450 at the then prevailing currency exchange rate. That is a little over $2,700 per measure or about $148,000 for each of the three written-on pages (both sides). But it would be wrong to apply this per-page arithmetic to the 80 surfaces of the *Requiem* autograph, even though it, like Christies' sale item, is an unfinished work. That calculation for the forty pages or 80 surfaces of the *Requiem* would bring the price only to $6,000,000. The *Requiem* has far more emotional value, to say nothing of its incredible provenance, than such a price would cover. A music lover or an institution might well pay $50,000,000 for it, maybe more. Its value as an investment can only improve over time. In fact, the work's original sale price, the details of which will be described shortly, was fifty ducats; looked at as an investment, appreciating over time, that compares favorably with $50,000,000. Of course, it is next to impossible to imagine a scenario by which the *Requiem* manuscript could ever be put up for sale.

Let us now review the state of affairs with respect to the manuscript of the *Requiem* immediately prior to the discovery of the score for delivery, supposedly in the gardener's cottage next to Stuppach Castle. Ironically, that cottage was not far away from the site of what had been Countess Wallsegg's tomb, and whose commission in 1791 along with that of the *Requiem* began this entire story.

The Austrian State Library already owned the last part of Mozart's original manuscript, namely surfaces nineteen through 80 of the autograph. It consisted of the music from the *Dies irae* to the conclusion of the *Hostias/Quam olim*, Mozart's last manuscript entry. In a way that is still unknown, the autograph, except for the first eighteen surfaces that had been made a part of the score for delivery, was divided up, probably after Süssmayr completed his work, and it wound up in the hands of two people.

Maximilian Stadler received that portion of the manuscript from the *Dies irae* up to and including the *Confutatis*. The remainder, from the *Lacrimosa* to the *Hostias/Quam olim*, became the property of Joseph Eybler. No one knows how these two men came into possession of the material, though Stadler could have received his portion as a gift from Constanze for his assistance to her over the years. Alternatively, Stadler simply could have helped himself to that piece of the manuscript while he was working on completions of certain movements of the *Requiem*. (Stadler's completions play no significant role in this story and, I do not know if they have ever been performed.)

But Eybler's possession of a piece of the manuscript is really a puzzle. The pages he owned were those containing all the sections of the *Requiem* on which he did *not* work; so he did not get the pages in order to retain an interest in his own completions. Following the abandonment of his commitment in early 1792, he must have returned the entire autograph to Constanze so that the next candidate could try his hand. Süssmayr obviously needed to have those pages in order to work on his own completion. It is conceivable, but unlikely, that Eybler kept the pages he eventually owned and later permitted Süssmayr access to them.

We must also assume that Constanze was unhappy at Eybler's withdrawal from the project. (It is, of course, possible that the circumstances were the other way round; that is, Süssmayr's alleged return from Kremsmünster Abbey in early 1792 triggered Eybler's withdrawal.) In any case, Constanze's state of mind towards Eybler is not consistent with a gift of appreciation, and it is unlikely that he received his pages from her. It is much more probable that he received them from Süssmayr at the time of the completion of the score for delivery. Perhaps Süssmayr wanted to thank Eybler for his ideas, many of which he incorporated into his completion.

One way or another, Stadler and Eybler owned all but the first eighteen surfaces of Mozart's original manuscript; we do not know how they got them, but we do know what they did with their two manuscript portions and when they did it.

In 1831, Stadler donated his pages of the manuscript to the Austrian National Library, and in 1833, Eybler did the same. Actually, his will stated an intention to donate his pages at the time of his death, but when Stadler died and Eybler had a stroke — both events occurring in 1833 — Eybler donated his part of the manuscript immediately, thirteen years before his death.

Thus we arrive at the year 1839 — some twelve years after Wallsegg's death — at the moment when the score for delivery was rediscovered. The Austrian National Library already held most of the original manuscript. However, the first eighteen surfaces —

about which the librarians had no knowledge — had been incorporated into the score for delivery.

As discussed above, in 1839 Nowack, at the request of Dietrichstein, was looking for six unknown Mozart string quartets in Stuppach. In his search, Nowack stumbled on the score for delivery and determined that it had, through four transfers of ownership, wound up in the hands of Katharina Adelpoller. (To remind the reader, ownership of the score went from Wallsegg to his sister following his death, to Joseph Leitner, to Karl Haag, and finally to Adelpoller.) How, why, and when something that ended up as Adelpoller's property was stored in the gardener's cottage — or even if that story is true — is an unfathomable mystery.

And what thoughts came to Nowack at the moment of discovery? What did he think he had found?

As well as he knew the *Requiem*'s history, when Nowack found Adelpoller's treasure, he thought that he had discovered the original manuscript of the entire *Requiem*, and all of it, he believed, completely in Mozart's hand.

His report to Dietrichstein — that is, a private letter — reads, "I should also inform your Excellency that among the ... papers [I examined] was the score for the *Requiem* that Mozart himself had prepared in 1792, signed, and turned over to Count Wallsegg. The handwriting is the same throughout the score, though it has been said that from the *Sanctus* or *Benedictus* on, it was written by Süssmayr."

It is clear that Nowack was confused about many details, including the date of Mozart's death, but at that time almost everyone was in a similar state of confusion. Nowack knew a good deal and, having been employed by Wallsegg, might have known more than most. Still, confusion reigned. One might think that on receiving Nowack's report via letter, Dietrichstein would have gone mad with joy. But a much more peculiar thing happened. He never got the letter, being absent from the library the day it arrived.

Instead, the news of the incredible discovery wound up on the desk of Dietrichstein's assistant, the library's curator, Ignaz Franz von Mosel, and it got there on or around November 1, 1838. The date is important because it enables one to determine just how casual Mosel was, and how long it took him to do anything about, what was arguably the most important news he would ever have occasion to deal with.

Nowack's letter to Dietrichstein, dated October 29, 1838, mailed from Stuppach on that day (which was a Monday), and traveling only 45 miles to Vienna by mail coach, was answered on November 13, 1838 (which was a Wednesday). In other words, Mosel took about two weeks to respond to the discovery. And then, with incredible *sang-froid*, when he responded, he suggested only that the manuscript be sent to him so that he could inspect it.

Meanwhile, not having received any response for his letter to Dietrichstein, Nowack went to Vienna on some other business, taking the score for delivery with him. Not knowing that his letter had been redirected to Mosel, Nowack went to Dietrichstein's house to show him what he had found.

Once again, Dietrichstein was not in and, in his absence, Nowack decided to show — and try to sell — the manuscript elsewhere. Tobias Haslinger, owner of a music store in Vienna, was offered the opportunity to buy a treasure. But did Haslinger reach for his wallet? No. He showed himself to be completely indifferent both to Nowack and to the manuscript.

Ultimately, contact was made between Nowack and Mosel, Dietrichstein finally returned, and serious negotiations started. Commenting on Adelpoller's asked-for and entirely reasonable price of fifty ducats — and the value of that in contemporary currency is very difficult to establish, probably less than a few hundred dollars U.S. — Dietrichstein remarked that he found it "rather excessive." Besides, argued the librarians, the *Requiem* had already been published in two editions. Therefore, they asserted, the value of the manuscript had become diminished. Nonetheless, the library would "graciously condescend" to buy the document as an "act of piety" to Mozart.

First, however, there had to be a serious investigation about the provenance of the autograph so as to assure the library that they would obtain clear title to it. Finally, on Christmas Eve day, 1838, the sale was completed — during the preliminary negotiations for which the 47th anniversary of Mozart's death passed, unheralded, as far as can be told.

On January 30, 1839, the following report was made public: "It has been confirmed that the complete original manuscript of the Mozart *Requiem* has been ... purchased by the [Austrian State Library]... This manuscript [is] *from the first to the last note* written by Mozart" [italics mine].

And the lengths to which the library would go to preserve this fiction introduces yet another party, Anton Herzog. However, Herzog's tale, a first-person account, presents an individual who was extremely important to the preservation of the history of the *Requiem*. At the time Herzog attempted publication of the history of the events that took place some 47 years earlier — and which would not influence our understanding of the *Requiem*'s story until the 1960s — he was a schoolteacher in the city of Wiener Neustadt, roughly halfway between Stuppach and Vienna. The tale describes his personal involvement with Wallsegg as well as the two performances of the work under the Count's direction in December 1793 and February 1794. Actually, Herzog did his work in two stages. The first stage was around 1827, when he gathered material by interviewing a number of people including Wallsegg himself, only two weeks before the Count died.

Because of Herzog's unwillingness to make public Wallsegg's deceptive behavior, he delayed publication of his findings for twelve years. Perhaps this decision was also to avoid public criticism of Constanze Mozart. In veiled language, but without specifically giving names, Herzog suggested that Wallsegg was treated shabbily. Only when the Austrian National Library purchased the score for delivery and then incorrectly declared it to be entirely in Mozart's hand did Herzog attempt to put his story into print.

The time of which Herzog writes — mostly the two-year period following Mozart's death — found him living near Stuppach and working as a teacher in one of the Count's schools. He also played both violin and viola in the Count's Tuesday and Thursday chamber music events.

According to his own words, he was a firsthand participant in almost everything associated with the two performances of the *Requiem* mounted by Wallsegg. In addition to playing with the orchestra, Herzog states that he "knew everything that happened in the office of the commissioner of the *Requiem*" (meaning Wallsegg, of course) and that he was asked by the Count to prepare the singers for the performances. However, as valuable as Herzog's history is, there is considerable difficulty in understanding it. His choice of words occasionally resulted in ambiguities at places where we need him to be the most precise. Furthermore, even he, with all his expertise and involvement, was both uncertain and incorrect about a number of important details.

For example, Herzog makes two extraordinary claims about the intimacy of his involvement with almost everything associated with the *Requiem*. First he says that he was present when "the transcript was made of the original score," and, second, that he (Herzog) had the "original score" in his possession for quite some time. The problem arises from the lack of uncertainty in the use of the words "original score."

While Herzog may have felt his statements to be perfectly clear, today it is impossible to grasp his meaning accurately. Wallsegg is said never to have shown the score for delivery (which is what we think of as the "original score") to anyone. It would not have been rational to do so, because that would expose the secret of authorship and show him to be falsely promoting himself as creator of music that he did not write. Instead, the Count is reputed to have taken the scores that he bought from various composers, and then to have personally prepared a copy of each score. He would only give the newly duplicated score to his copyist, Johann Bernard, to prepare performance parts for the individual orchestral instruments and singers. In fact, elsewhere in his extraordinary history, Herzog says, "[I] never saw an original score." Thus, it is impossible to be sure what documents he is referring to and which artifacts he alleges to have seen, the score for delivery or Wallsegg's handmade copy of it. Later, his report clarifies this particular ambiguity to some degree, but it is difficult to construct a completely cohesive story from his narrative. There are many other examples of ambiguities in his history as well.

It appears that Herzog began thinking about capturing the details of the *Requiem*'s history at the time of the great scandal initiated by Weber. But a greater motivation was derived from Maximilian Stadler's 1826 rebuttal to Weber in defense of the *Requiem*'s authenticity. While Herzog praises Stadler's work, reading between the lines we may come to sense that Herzog recognized errors in Stadler's description of some details. It sounds strange to suggest that a young man living near Stuppach would know more about the *Requiem*'s true history than someone getting information from Mozart's widow. But the fact is that Herzog was better placed than Stadler.

For example, the musicians in Wallsegg's orchestra must have known about his little conceit, though they may not have known the names of the composers who supplied Wallsegg with compositions. Certainly, Herzog suggests that Wallsegg's secret was well known by the players. Unless musicians today behave in radically different ways from those in the 1700s, we can freely assume they gossiped about Wallsegg's little game. Herzog therefore had a good understanding of the flaws in Stadler's story, and he set about to give a more accurate one.

Among Herzog's sources was Wallsegg himself. Unfortunately, while the Count could speak definitively about his role in the scheme, he was either unwilling or unqualified to speak about the material he received from Constanze; bear in mind, after all, that he, himself, had been deceived about the manuscript's authenticity. The fact is that Herzog did not get a great deal of accurate information from Wallsegg except, perhaps, some background detail. Mostly, what interested Herzog was the matter of the disputed sections, the *Sanctus, Benedictus, Agnus Dei*, and to a lesser extent, the *Lacrimosa*, and this was data about which Wallsegg knew little if anything. By the time the Count died, Herzog had the basic story documented, but because he knew that it would damage Wallsegg's reputation, he decided to keep silent on the matter.

When, in 1839, the Austrian National Library made its announcement about finding the score of the *Requiem* in Stuppach, explicitly stating that it was entirely in Mozart's hand, Herzog decided to set the record straight. He wrote up the story and tried to get it published. However, the library had much greater political influence than Herzog, and, forewarned by library officials after reading his material, Austrian censors refused to allow its publication. Had Herzog waited a few years before submitting his story, the situation might have been different. But to challenge the library's announcement immediately was too much. His report, entitled "The true and detailed history of the Requiem of W.A. Mozart from its origin in the year 1791 to the present period in 1839. By Anton Herzog, Director of the district High School and Choirmaster in Wiener Neustadt," was forbidden publication.

The author of the first substantive Mozart biography, Otto Jahn, knew of the report, but he did not mention it in his 1856-59 history of the composer. Apparently, the situation was still an open wound. Not until 1923 was an edited version of the report printed in a Viennese newspaper. Other edited and unedited versions of Herzog's report were made available at later dates.

Reading Herzog's entire report, it becomes clear why some published English language versions of it are edited. Some parts of Herzog's material simply cannot be understood. Worse, there are parts presented as fact that contain data that is worse than incredible. The information is bizarre.

For example, Herzog asserts that "the manuscript [of the *Requiem*] that was kept at Leipzig" (referring to the one used by Breitkopf & Härtel for the *Requiem*'s first printed edition in 1800) had a different *Agnus Dei* than the one in the possession of Wallsegg.

In explanation of this grave factual error, Herzog gives a complicated and unbelievable story about Wallsegg claiming to be a pupil of Mozart, and writing his own *Agnus Dei* with Mozart examining and correcting it by post. Even accepting Wallsegg as eccentric in his use of other musician's compositions, this story is so fantastic that it drifts from the incomprehensible to the impossible, and represents the kind of thing that has been edited out of some published versions of Herzog's story.

In 1838, with all pages of the *Requiem* manuscript now in one location for the first time since 1792, the Viennese library reassembled the three formerly separate sections of the autograph. With its first eighteen surfaces removed, the score for delivery, as it exists today, begins with the *Dies irae*. In 1991, a facsimile edition of the *Requiem* was printed containing both Mozart's manuscript and the torso of what is, ironically, the score for delivery.

A FESTIVAL OF MISFORTUNES AND DEATH

The telling of the tale of the Mozart *Requiem* finds, at every turn in the journey and with almost every person pivotally associated with it, either some dimension of human misfortune or else a direct alliance with death. The work seems to have touched those involved in its development with adversity.

Of course, the central motivation for its creation was the sudden and tragic death of Countess Wallsegg. And Mozart's creation of it was accompanied by premonitions of his own death, its completion prevented in reality by his passing.

Joseph Eybler, the person who first agreed to complete the unfinished torso (but who failed to do so) forever lost what should have been a critical place in the history of the composition. And during a performance of the work, conducted by him in 1833, he suffered a paralyzing stoke and never fully recovered.

Franz Xaver Süssmayr, whose *Requiem* completion has been performed for more than two centuries, was never given a suitable

141

acknowledgment for the effort while he lived. Instead, the party who should have been eternally grateful to him, Mozart's widow, misrepresented his efforts and contributions. Süssmayr died of tuberculosis aggravated by chronic alcoholism, and ever since has been pilloried as having been inadequate for the task. On top of that, he is accused of being a plagiarist who stole from Mozart. Further, almost certainly spurious allegations about a sexual relationship between him and Mozart's wife have all been offered without reliable evidence, besmirching both of their reputations to this day.

The *deus ex machina* of the *Requiem*, Count Wallsegg, derived little pleasure from commissioning Mozart to write the work. He was cheated and swindled by Constanze; he lost all control of something over which he was supposed to have had exclusive ownership; and eventually he even let slip away from him the physical manifestation of his commission, specifically the manuscript score for delivery. The irony of his involvement is that, had it not been for Constanze's duplicitous conduct towards him, we almost certainly would have forever lost Mozart's final and remarkable musical testament. Several people in Mozart's life were honored by a performance of the *Requiem* at the time of their deaths, but Wallsegg was never given that consideration.

The reputation of Mozart's widow was seriously injured by her behavior with respect to the *Requiem*'s completion following Mozart's death, to say nothing of unfounded allegations about her faithlessness to Mozart and the parentage of her last child, Franz Xaver Wolfgang Mozart. There do not seem to have been any signs, preceding her husband's death, to predict a significant change in personality, but after December 5, 1791, Constanze appears to have shifted from a shy, quiet, retiring housewife to a strong-willed, deceitful woman.

As for Jacob Weber, his attacks on the authenticity of the *Requiem* ruined what was otherwise his own well-deserved reputation. Various defenses of the work were published to contradict his polemical article and they cast him in a very poor light.

Only when Karl Mozart, the last known living descendant of the composer, died unmarried and without known issue, and whose journey to an eternal rest — like that of his previously deceased mother and brother — was accompanied by his father's final composition, did the tragedy and death surrounding the *Requiem* loosen its grip.

Who, then, was well served by the commissioning and production of the *Requiem*, this veritable festival of death whose final form is that of an incomplete torso? The answer to that question is simple. It is the world that benefited, continues to benefit, and will benefit every time the sublime work is performed.

CONTEMPORARY SÜSSMAYRS

One can argue, and with ample supportive evidence, that Süssmayr's completion contains many serious technical flaws. That audiences have enjoyed his completion of the Mozart *Requiem* for more than two centuries without being distressed by those infelicities speaks more to the training of the listeners than to the implied unimportance of the deficiencies. Some of them can be demonstrated without any necessity for detailed technical analysis, and a few of these cases were cited above. Others cannot be discussed without resorting to specialized terminology and they are well presented elsewhere.

Given that Süssmayr's completion does have problems, other musicians, composers, scholars, teachers, theoreticians, and performers have attempted to complete the *Requiem* again many times since 1792. At least one doctoral candidate's dissertation documented and contrasted all known completions. Some have tried to retain Süssmayr's basic structure, design, and content so as to present a completion that an audience will not find abrasive to their already preconditioned ears. Others take a fresh start.

Completions by the Dutch composer and Mozart scholar, the late Marius Flothuis, as well as that of the late Karl Marguerre need to be mentioned. Flothuis' work is not so much a new completion as a fix-up of some of the orchestrational difficulties in Süssmayr's completion. Specifically, he corrected some elements of Süssmayr's clumsy orchestration, made the Osanna fugue longer, and changed the key of the fugue that follows the *Benedictus* so that it agrees with the same fugue as it appears following the *Sanctus*. Following Marguerre's death in 1981, his daughter, Charlotte Heath Marguerre, effected a revision of his completion.

The earliest of the five contemporary and published completions is that of the German musicologist Franz Beyer and published by Edition Kunzelmann. This may be the most frequently performed of all contemporary completions. What Beyer did was to eliminate problems in Süssmayr's orchestral accompaniment, that is, every section except the *Requiem aeternam*, which was completed almost entirely by Mozart. However, problems found in the choral parts of the *Sanctus/Osanna*, *Benedictus/Osanna*, *Agnus Dei*, and the *Lacrimosa* were not similarly repaired in his edition. This was probably deliberate because, had such changes been implemented, every chorus that takes part in a performance of the work would need to purchase new vocal scores, which would substantially increase the cost associated with the mounting of any performance of the *Requiem*. Even so, Beyer's work presents the *Requiem* in a much more satisfactory form than Süssmayr's, despite the structural infelicities that still remain. For example, he did not enlarge the too-short *Osanna* fugues to a more appropriate length. Beyer certainly was concerned to avoid creating an edition that would jar the ear of those familiar with the well-known Süssmayr version, and to avoid requiring an already trained chorus to learn a substantially new version.

An edition of the work by the English scholar Dr. Richard Maunder of Oxford University received a great deal of attention at the time it was first made available. Oxford University Press publishes it, as well as Maunder's book on the problems inherent in making a new edition of the *Requiem*. There are several distinct elements of Maunder's effort, one of which is a completion of the

Amen fugue spoken of earlier. A critical decision in his reworking of the *Requiem* was the elimination of both the *Sanctus/Osanna* and *Benedictus/Osanna* sections. In his acceptance of the view that these two movements have nothing to do with Mozart, he suggested that they be dropped from performance. However, in doing so he reintroduced at least a part of the problem that Süssmayr had eliminated, namely, that the *Requiem* as left by Mozart is too short for the religious purposes it is intended to serve. On the other hand, Maunder retains the *Agnus Dei* because of his belief that the movement has Mozartean substance (an assertion that is very much open to debate).

Two completions of the *Requiem* were commissioned for different circumstances, one for performance at the 1984 York Festival in England, commissioned by Peter Seymour and the Yorkshire Bach Choir, and the other for performance in 1991 as part of the events surrounding the bicentennial of Mozart's death. The English musician, composer, and teacher, Duncan Druce, did the completion for York. It offers the most radical edition because Druce did not feel himself constrained to use the Süssmayr movements to the extent of other completers. For example, in addition to his completion of the *Amen* fugue, Druce's *Sanctus, Benedictus,* and *Agnus Dei*, while having similarities to Süssmayr's sections, are in fact newly composed works. (Neither the published score, by Novello, nor the recording of Druce's edition, contain his later and completely recomposed *Agnus Dei*.) He also recognized the major flaw in the brevity of Süssmayr's first *Osanna* fugue of only 27 measures, and corrected the problem by introducing one that is more than twice as long, a length that provides the dignity and breadth required of the religious thought supporting the words, "Hosanna in the highest."

The American composer, scholar, teacher, theorist, and concert pianist Robert D. Levin of Harvard University took a middle of the road, conservative position. He retained the familiarity of the Süssmayr edition while simultaneously eliminating all the infelicities of the original completion, both orchestral and vocal. His publication contains a completion of the *Amen* fugue, but he did that part of work years earlier. Levin's edition, formerly published by Hänssler-Verlag of Stuttgart has been taken over by Carus Verlag, also of Stuttgart, and has been recorded on several occasions.

The completion by the American musicologist H.C. Robbins Landon consists of a conflation of Eybler's work with Süssmayr's. It, like the previous four, has been published and recorded. This makes it possible to hear Eybler's approach, which contains many solutions to the completion problem that differ from those of Süssmayr.

The year 2006 is the quarter millennium celebration of Mozart's birth; worldwide celebrations are sure to feature the *Requiem* in many forms. Music of this caliber draws crowds even in remote settlements, and ironically, brings joy even while resonating with the mourning of death. Musicians as well as audiences remain awed by it Even incomplete, damaged, and with the awkward infelicities found in the Süssmayr edition, it is an overpowering musical and emotional experience to take any part in a performance of the Mozart *Requiem*.

In The Requiem's Healing Embrace

When a tragedy occurs, we frequently use the solace, consolation, and curative powers of great music as a balm for recuperation. In western civilization, at least, more often than is realized, that balm takes the form of a performance of the Mozart *Requiem*.

For example, following the war in the Balkans in the 1990s, the surviving members of the Sarajevo Philharmonic were gathered together to give a performance of the *Requiem* in the midst of the rubble of the city. It was at that moment that Sarajevo began to be reborn.

In Germany, the *Requiem* has been played in Dresden's Frauenkirche on the anniversary of that city's bombardment by Allied forces every year since 1945.

In France, the *Requiem* was played on December 15, 1840 when Napoleon's body was placed in the Church of Saint-Louis des Invalides in Paris after having been moved from Saint-Helena Island. A Paris newspaper report of the event stated that, following the funeral service, "Mozart's magnificent *Requiem*, that supreme lamentation, appropriate to all misfortunes, that song of mourning and triumph, where experience and despair mingle in a sacred way, was sung and executed by the greatest artists of France, because they, too, wanted to pay their tribute and respect to the great Emperor."

On January 19, 1964, following the assassination of President John F. Kennedy, a nationally televised performance of the *Requiem* was given at Boston's Cathedral of the Holy Cross. Richard Cardinal Cushing celebrated a solemn pontifical requiem mass in memory of the fallen president.

Commemorating the tragic events of September 11, 2001, the Seattle Symphony, under the direction of Gerard Schwarz, gave a concert performance of the *Requiem* in January 2002. Following the concert, one of the chorus members had a chance encounter with an anonymous patron. "Wouldn't it be great," the supporter said, "if somehow all the best choruses could join together and ring the area around Ground Zero? You could all sing the *Requiem* in honor of those who died. There'd surely be enough of you to represent a voice for each one lost." And from that inspiration, the Seattle Symphony Chorale developed what came to be called "The Rolling *Requiem*."

On September 11, 2002, in 20 of the earth's 24 time zones, between 180 and 210 performances of the Mozart *Requiem* (or sections of it) took place — several cities had multiple performances given by different organizations and in unrelated locations. A few chose another composition appropriate to the emotions of the occasion, for example, the beautiful and memorable "*Requiem*" of Gabriel Fauré. All of this involved more than 18,000 people in 25 countries. Beginning in New Zealand, in time zone 24, west of the International Dateline, the commemorative events traveled westward with the final performances occurring in American Samoa, located in time zone 1, east of the International Dateline. Many performances began at exactly 8:46 a.m., corresponding to the time of the first attack on the World Trade Center. While every performance was noteworthy, a few were made especially memorable by the unique and stirring local circumstances. In Pardubice, Czechoslovakia, for example, the State Philharmony was accompanied by the combined resources of the ten best choirs from the entire Czech Republic for a performance of the Mozart *Requiem*.

In Seattle, Washington, so many wished to hear the performance that the venue was changed to Safeco Field, the Seattle Mariner's baseball stadium. There, the world-class Seattle Symphony Orchestra centered itself on second base with the chorus in shallow center field.

The 51 people isolated at the South Pole's Amundsen-Scott Research Center had neither a chorus nor an orchestra. However, they played a recorded performance — which was heard in all of the earth's times zones at once.

A list of locales that participated in this global performance of the *Requiem* is given in the Appendix. How arresting that the emotions of a sorrowful husband over the death of his wife, as imagined by Mozart and those who completed his work, were made manifest in such an event.

EPILOGUE: A FICTION STORY

In the prologue, a brief story dating from before the Civil War was given as an example of the kind of romantic literature about Mozart and the *Requiem* that thrived during the nineteenth century and into the twentieth century. Here, another remarkable story, dating from the July/September 1850 issue of *Living Age* (printed by E. Littell & Company, Philadelphia & New York, itself a reprint from the May 1850 English periodical, *Fraser's Magazine*) acts as a bookend.

Living Age had no journalistic theme, but offered stories varying from, for example, a report of a "New and Extraordinary Printing Machine" exhibited in Paris, to poetry by one Mrs. Stephen Lushington, to a story about "The Arctic Experience." The Mozart fable here is more precise than the first one given, though it contains a number of name peculiarities and misspellings. For example, the librettist for Mozart's Opera, *The Clemency of Titus*, is given as "Maroli" instead of "Mazzolà, the name of the bird catcher in Mozart's opera, *The Magic Flute* is given as "Paragon" instead of "Papageno," and Süssmayr's name is spelled as Süssmayer.

The story presents an invented and unique view of Mozart's death, an absolutely singular variation of the assassination theory. Here, a central figure named "Hofer" (whose first name is never given), believes himself partly responsible for Mozart's death. The character bears the same family name as a person from Mozart's real life, the violinist Franz de Paula Hofer, related to Mozart by way of Hofer's marriage to Mozart's sister-in-law, Josepha. Even more, the details of the story's Hofer demonstrate some similarities to the real-life Hofer.

The fictional Hofer is made a cousin of the real-life husband of Mozart's older sister, Maria Anna Wallburga Ignatia Mozart, nicknamed "Nannerl." Hofer's profession in this story is that of a music copyist. A brief, passing mention to yet a third Hofer is found in the story by way of mention of the "Tell of the Tyrol," the reference being to Andreas Hofer, a non-fictional Tirolese patriot and popular nineteenth-century romantic hero who was involved in an unsuccessful rebellion against Napoleon.

Masterminding the actions of the fictional Hofer and creating a plan to take advantage of the belief that Mozart was wildly superstitious is the *deus ex machina* of the story, Johann Joseph Schickaneder, nicknamed Emanuel, the real-life librettist of Mozart's opera, *The Magic Flute*. Other real-life characters mentioned in the story include clarinetist Anton Stadler, "Shack," probably *The Magic Flute's* original Tamino, Benedikt Schack (who is said to have sung sections from the *Requiem* eleven hours before Mozart's death), and "Gorl," probably *The Magic Flute's* original Sarastro, Franz Gerle (who also participated in the deathbed singing of the *Requiem*).

The story begins innocently enough at a tavern in Prague, where a character speaks about Mozart's visit to that city during the performances of *The Clemency of Titus,* which took place in 1791. In making a statement about the origin of the *Requiem,* the character is interrupted by a stranger seated at a nearby table who contradicts his story. Here things turn grim, and eventually we get a story-within-a-story about the circumstances of Mozart's death. The text is a mixture of English and American spellings, all of which have been retained as originally printed.

The account offers conjectures that now add another item to the already long list of theoretical causes of Mozart's death. The conclusion is chilling.

The Story of "The Requiem"

Author: anonymous
Published in Boston in 1850
By E. Littell & Company

In the year 1816, an Englishman of the name of Vaughan was residing in the city of Prague, where he had been induced to settle for several years, from the liking that he felt for the ancient Bohemian capital, and the advantages that it offered to a gentleman in straitened circumstances.

Vaughan was a man of studious and retired habits, not fond of general society, but not unwilling to seek the friendship of those in whom he expected to find talent, originality, learning, or knowledge of the world. Having no domestic circle of any kind to attract him to his lodgings at meal times, he was in the habit of dining at a coffeehouse bearing the title of *Der Adler,* and kept by a man by the name of Hunten.

This man was a large, lumpy, but intelligent German; his father had kept the house before him, and his great pride was to speak of the day when he himself, then a boy of eight years old, had heard with his own ears the voice of the great Mozart hum some of the magic music of the *Zauberflöte,* one of the operas that the great composer gave to the world during the last few months of his life.

On this subject Hunten was inexhaustible. He had several pictures of Mozart in his coffee-room; he had a pocket handkerchief of the great Wolfgang, bequeathed to him by his father, as a sacred and precious relic; and he also possessed a toothpick, of the same great interest to the artist world — an article, however, never shown to the profane, and only mentioned and exhibited to such as felt the importance of the valuable object, and who never divulged what their eyes had seen, and their hands had touched, to any person likely to laugh at it or them.

Hunten's enthusiasm made him well known to the tourists and inhabitants who visited or resided in Prague; and Vaughan often amused himself with setting Hunten astride on his hobby, and letting him ride thereon for an indefinite space of time.

One wet evening in the month of November, Vaughan had gone to the coffee-house to dine, and had staid there longer than usual, talking with some of the strangers who had come in, and who were discussing the affairs of the recent war, as the news that the city itself afforded was meagre and threadbare by six o'clock in the afternoon.

Hunton was standing near listening and joining in the conversation, and trusting that some happy turn in the discourse might give him the wished-for opportunity of introducing his recollections of Mozart, when this desire was unexpectedly granted by a young German traveller observing that he believed Bonaparte, by that time a captive on the rock, to be the evil one incarnate, and as such not likely to remain long in confinement.

"*Bah!*" said a Frenchman, who believed in nothing but what he smelled, saw, tasted, or touched.

"*Comment!*" cried the German.

"Bah! vous me dites. Bah! Monsieur."

"*Bêtise! si vous le préférez.*" The German rose, but Hunten interposed.

"Messieurs, ici on mange, on boit, on cause, mais on ne se bât pas."

"*Vous avez raison,*" said the good-humored little Gaul.

"Ah, gentlemen, I could tell you that it is not impossible that the evil one may be incarnate. I have heard of such things. Remember the story of the 'Requiem,'" said Hunten.

"Ah! tell us about that," said Duclos.

"*Volontiers!*" said Hunten, with heartfelt cheerfulness. "You all know, gentlemen, that the evil one appeared to Mozart, and told him three times to write a Requiem!"

"*Vraiment!*" said Duclos.

"It is an undoubted fact," said Hunten. "Once he came, this stranger in black, before Mozart left Vienna for Prague in 1791. He came, gentlemen, to write an opera for the coronation of Emperor Leopold. The Bohemian nobility chose the subject, and it was the

'Clemency of Titus.' Titus was a Roman emperor, gentlemen, son of Nero, of whom you may have heard. The story is affecting, and was penned by Marroli, the court poet. Here in Prague it was performed; and I had the honor of attending at a party at Monsieur Duflek's, where some admirable music was to be heard, even outside the door; which, gentlemen, was my post that night, for it was in the character of additional attendant at the supper-table that I appeared at Monsieur Duflek's. Once while he was at Prague, the great Mozart saw the stranger in black."

"No! he did not," said a voice near.

"How, sir?" said Hunten, turning sharply round.

Vaughan saw a man sitting a few yards from him at a small table, on which lay the fragments of a biscuit and half a glass of hermitage. The man's face was only partially lighted by the lamp that hung above his head, and the fire-light, that flashed fitfully and uncertainly on the circle who had gathered round the chimney corner.

"How, sir?" repeated Hunten.

"He did *not*," repeated the stranger; and after having repeated these words he tossed off his wine and walked out of the coffee-room.

"Who is that?" said Vaughan.

"That man's name is Hofer."

"What! the Tell of the Tyrol?" said Duclos, laughing.

"Not that I am aware of," said Hunten. "He is a cousin of the man who married Mozart's sister. Hofer sang in the opera at Vienna; but this young man was brought up in Spain, and never so much as saw Mozart, as far as I know."

"Then how could he speak so positively!" asked Vaughan.

"I do not know. But to return to Mozart," said Hunten; "we saw him at Prague in September. He left us at the end of the month, and returned to fresh glories in Vienna. He had not been long returned when again the mysterious stranger appeared, and requested a private audience with the composer. No one knows what passed — no one will ever know in this world, gentlemen; but from that hour Mozart drooped and pined, and he wrote the sublime music of the 'Requiem,' knowing that it would be his farewell to his art. On the 5th of December his friends, Shack, Hofer, and Gorl, assembled in his room, and round his dying bed arose the strains that will confer on him a glorious immortality! There the angels might have listened to harmonies pure and sublime as the heavenly hallelujahs. The stranger's mission had been fulfilled — Mozart's 'Requiem' was his last work."

"*Bêtise!*" said the Frenchman.

"*Ist es Möglich?*" said the German.

Vaughan asked where Hofer lived. Hunten replied that he believed he had changed his abode lately, and mentioned the name of his last one. He added, that he believed Hofer supported himself by copying music and manuscripts for the librarians and the artists in the town.

Vaughan felt a great desire to become acquainted with this man, and endeavored to procure his address from a shop to which Hunten directed him. The bookseller to whom he applied gave him the address that he wished for, and Vaughan hastened to the street therein designated; but on arriving there he was much disappointed to find that Hofer had gone to the country on business, having been engaged by a certain Count Platen to make a list of his library, and to copy out some family manuscripts that he did not choose to remove from the castle where they always lay.

It was said that Hofer was to return in three weeks, probably; but a month had elapsed before Vaughan saw or heard anything of him. About the new year time there was to be a concert at Prague, for which some of the best Viennese performers had been engaged. The entertainment was to consist entirely of Mozart's music, sacred and profane.

The first part was to commence with the overture to *Don Giovanni*. This was to be followed by the quintet "Sento o Dio!" from the *Così fan tutti*; and the rest of the part was to be filled by pieces chosen from his most admired works. The second portion was to begin with the "Lacrimosa," and other parts of the *Requiem*. It was to be followed by the "Kyrie Eleison," and "Gloria in excelsis" of the twelfth mass. Other fragments of sacred music were to succeed and the whole was to conclude with the "Bless the Lord" from a manuscript mass.

Vaughan went to this concert, and being one of those who detest attending such an entertainment with a party of friends, he went early and alone, and, establishing himself in one of the best places, waited patiently until the performance should begin.

The first bar of the sublime "Sento o Dio!" was swelling on the ear of Vaughan, when he heard at his right-hand the words whispered —

"Ach! Himmel ich" —

The person who uttered them had intended, he supposed, to state that she was going to faint, for this she did before another second had elapsed. She fell heavily forward, and Vaughan immediately raised her up, and naturally expected to find that the young girl would be claimed by some relation or chaperone, as she could not, he supposed, have come alone and unattended into so great a crowd. On looking round, however, he saw that no one appeared to take any particular interest in her, and he soon found that none had the least intention of occupying themselves with her; so far, at least, as to volunteer their services to take her from the room, through a crowd that she would find it impossible to pass without some strong arm to assist her progress. Vaughan had a natural loving-kindness of disposition that would have led him to help any human being, however humble or insignificant, in a time of distress, and he at once made up his mind to offer his assistance to the young girl, who recovered in a few minutes sufficiently to walk with the support of his arm, to the entrance nearest to the places they had both occupied. The girl was about fifteen, and, from her dress and appearance, must belong, Vaughan thought, to the middling class. Her father might be a merchant, a prosperous tradesman, an artist, or a master of music or languages. She had taken Vaughan's arm without any hesitation, as she was only anxious, apparently, to get out of the over-heated saloon as quickly as possible. When she reached the fresh, cool vestibule, she sighed as if relieved, and said, in a pretty-toned voice, "*Ich danke ihnen! ich danke ihnen!*" and, wrapping a hood over her head, she prepared to leave the hall. She stopped short, however, with a look of disappointment when she discovered that it was snowing. Vaughan asked her in German whether she had a servant or a carriage in attendance. "*Nein, nein!*" she replied, hurriedly. Vaughan represented to her that the snow was falling fast, and that she was not in a fit state to make her way alone through the wet streets. She appeared very much disturbed by this advice, and, after one or two attempts at speech, she burst out crying. Vaughan suspected that for some reason she had come to the concert without telling her friends, and, feeling some pity and concern for the pain incurred by a youthful frolic, he at once made up his mind to get a conveyance as quickly as he could and send the child home, paying the fare himself, for he had found out that one of the principal causes of her distress was not having a cent in her pocket. The vehicle was ready for her in two minutes, and, as Vaughan was to pay the expenses, it was necessary that she should divulge the street and number of her dwelling. She did so with considerable trepidation, and Vaughan, after paying the man, returned to the concert-room, determined to find out next day the name and circumstances of the young lady whom he had befriended that night. He went back to his place and came in for the *Prenderò quel brunettino*. As the duet concluded an old lady, of a cheerful countenance, in an orange-colored satin, and wielding a large Spanish fan, leaned forward, and, tapping Vaughan on the elbow, said —

"Is she better?"

"Yes," said Vaughan, "and gone home. May I ask," he added, "if you know her name?"

"*Gewiss;* Teresa Hofer."

"*Wie,*" cried Vaughan.

The old lady was an affable being, who delighted in giving information. She told Vaughan that Teresa Hofer was the daughter of a man employed by her son to copy music for the orchestra of his theatre; that she had seen the said Teresa when she herself had gone on messages to and from Hofer's house on her son's affairs. She then diverged into an account of her son's prospects in life, the dissipated habits of his second violin, and the gross neglect of rehearsals by the first clarinet; and she pointed to the two individuals who were perched in conspicuous places on the platform before them. Vaughan asked a few questions about Hofer; but the old lady knew nothing about him beyond his merits as a diligent and correct copyist, and with this information Vaughan was obliged to content himself.

When the second part began Vaughan listened with awful and solemnizing pleasure to the tremendous music of the "Requiem." The well-known tale of the stranger's visits to Mozart returned to his mind. The prophetic gloom of a death-boding presentiment had lain heavy on the soul of the great composer when that music of unearthly power had flowed through his brain.

He left the room on its conclusion, not wishing to lay any other sensation above it; and he walked home in a clear, keen starlight. The snow-clouds had cleared off, and high rode the moon, with a sharp, bright face, turned full on the streets through which he passed. His thoughts were still with the "Requiem" and its composer; and he endeavored to define to himself his own belief with respect to the supernatural warning attached to the origin of Mozart's great and final work.

It was not an illusion; the stranger had appeared in the body, that was certain. What means had he used to impress Mozart so deeply? or was it rather the morbid and diseased imagination of the musician that had distorted a plain and common incident into a supernatural warning and prophetic visitation? He could not decide this point to his own satisfaction, and he felt an increasing desire to become acquainted with the man Hofer, who, from his connection by marriage with Mozart, very probably would know some circumstances not generally revealed to strangers, and which had not, therefore, found their way into the mouths of the public.

Next day but one he went to Hofer's under pretence of getting some music copied, and waited until Hofer was able to see him. Then being introduced into his parlor, he saw sitting at a writing table the young girl Teresa, whom he had assisted the evening before in the concert-room. She looked up and smiled; and when Hofer entered, she spoke to him in German and announced Vaughan as her hero and deliverer. Hofer thanked him for his kindness and attention, and explained that he had been away from home, and that his daughter, having been left under the jurisdiction of an old female relation, had been refused the pleasure of attending the concert, the old relation herself being cross and stingy. That at the last hour Teresa had determined to go, on being offered a ticket, ten minutes before the concert began, by a friend who found himself unable to attend. Teresa had not been able to find a companion going to that part of the concert-room, in so short a notice at least, and she had set off hurriedly alone, knowing that she would not obtain leave to go if she asked it, but resolved on hearing the music at any price.

Hofer thanked Vaughan cordially for taking care of the little Teresa; and the Englishman then produced the music that he wished to have transposed into another key, for the use of a friend to whom he meant to send it.

Vaughan was very well disposed to stay and converse with the copyist after the business on which he had come had been discussed, for there was in the manner, and voice, and face of Hofer a power of attracting and fixing the attention, of which Vaughan could hardly define the cause, though he deeply felt the effect.

Vaughan, however, rightly assigned some part of the influence possessed by this stranger to the remarkable and picturesque appearance that age had not deprived of its romantic charms. The hair was gray, but it fell over a brow and shaded a head of heroic form; the eyes were deeply set, and the dark blue color from its depth gave them the intensity of black; the complexion was pale olive, and the *tout ensemble* flashed full on you, at different moments, like a breathing Velasquez — so Spanish was the coloring of the whole countenance, and so stately the figure of the poor copyist, whose claims to noble descent were but slender, to judge from appearances.

Vaughan found in Hofer an agreeable companion on further acquaintance. He experienced little difficulty in obtaining an intimate footing in his house, and as months passed on he spent more and more of his time in his society. He used to go to Hofer's house in the evenings, and sit for an hour or two; and he endeavored on all occasions to find out what was the meaning of the abrupt exclamation to which Hofer had given vent at the coffee-house on the occasion of their first meeting. Hofer, however, always replied that he had said it in jest, to make people stare, and that he knew very little of Mozart, though he was a cousin of the man who had married the composer's sister. Vaughan saw at last that he could get no other explanation, and asked no more questions on a subject which he could see gave ill-concealed annoyance to the other party concerned.

Their friendship lasted, however, unbroken by absence or other causes, for the space of three years; and it was with sincere regret that Vaughan saw in Hofer, at the end of that time, some symptoms of the return of an illness with which he knew that he had once been afflicted, and which was, he feared, very likely to put a painful and sudden end to his days.

One evening, when Vaughan had been sitting beside the couch where the German lay for a considerable time, he fell into the musing mood that loves a long space of silent twilight, wherein to dream itself calmly out undisturbed by the external world. The sick man had fallen asleep. Vaughan had promised the young girl Teresa that he would watch at the side of her father while she went out to execute some household commissions, and as he sat waiting her return his thoughts returned to the object that had first excited his inquiries about the poor man who lay dying beside him. Vaughan's taste for music was so strong, that it accompanied every thought, every idea, that sprung up in his rapid and desultory mind. A thousand different melodies would pass over his brain in an hour or two, without his being conscious of effort; and every phase of feeling — grave, or gay, or pensive — found for him an expression in some one of the melodies from the vast magazine of his musical memory.

All his thoughts had turned towards Mozart on the evening in question. His love for the music of the great master amounted to a passion, and often had he sat, as he did at that moment, wrapped in the silken memory of his loveliest harmonies, and following, with reverent and inquiring sympathy, the sublime spirit to its everlasting future as anxiously as if the two had been firm friends parted, and longing for reunion after death. His admiration for the master had warmed into love for the individual being, and to penetrate into the cheerless mystery that shrouded the latter days of the departed genius had become an object of painful anxiety to Vaughan.

For years past he had accustomed himself to collect all the noblest passages in prose or poetry which had music and the mystery of musical temperament for their subject. This employment had pleased his wild fancy, and he had collected flowers enough to form the rarest garland — flowers of every hue, from the superb gravity of Hooker to the rollicking rhymes of less reverend writers on the pleasures of music — and that evening there sailed into his mind, swiftly one after the other, a strange and motley fleet from the enchanted land of song, conveyed by the stern memory of one of his first and favorite quotations: —

"In harmony the very image and character, even of virtue and vice, is perceived — the mind delighted with their resemblances, and brought, by having them often iterated, into a love of the things themselves. For which there is nothing more contagious and pestilent than some kinds of harmony; than some, nothing more strong and potent unto good. There is that draweth to a marvellous grave and sober mediocrity; there is also that carrieth, as it were, into ecstasies, filling the mind with an heavenly joy, and for the time in a manner severing it from the body."

And as these words passed through Vaughan's memory, the thought to which they gave rise melted into melody, and from his half-closed lips emerged faintly the angel air of the "Lacrimosa."—

The inexpressible and tender mournfulness of the measure damped the eyelids of Vaughan with the mere memory of its beauty, and he continued to rehearse it in a low tone to himself; but his voice strengthened in spite of himself, and he clearly defined the graceful crest of the passage that crowns, as it were, the whole of the quartet with glorious name of the Lord.

"*Pie Jesu Domine,*" faintly replied the voice of the dying Hofer, in a tone that was not music, but its shadow.

Vaughan turned quickly round, and looked at the figure that lay beneath his eyes. The eyes were half-closed, the hands were clasped; but by the quivering of the lids the emotion of the invalid might be seen.

"I fear I have disturbed you," said Vaughan.

"No, said Hofer, after a moment's pause; "you have not. I was not sleeping. I was wondering whether it was worth while to tell you a strange passage in my history, one which I would wish heartily at this hour to efface."

"Connected with the composer?" said Vaughan, drawing near.

"Yes!" said Hofer, raising himself on his elbow, and looking intently in Vaughan's face. "This is the first evening that I have ever felt disposed to speak of this subject to you. It is a strange and rare thing, the story of the 'Requiem.' You know the tale that has gone about the world of the supernatural circumstances attending the death of the great Mozart. It was fitting that he should have a death-bed decorated with other garniture than what belongs to those of most men, and he had it. His spirit ascended amid the incense that he himself had prepared and laid on the altar of God's praise. They stood around him, the faithful friends of festive days, and they crowned the dying genius with his own glory ere he departed. Do you not think that ascension was winged with a rapture as divine as that which filled the heart of the prophet in the fire-chariot of ancient Israel?"

"Yet he wept," said Vaughan.

"Yes," said Hofer, with wild and serious eyes fixed on the face of the Englishman. "Yes, he wept — true. Not with the awful joy of the dying believer. I will tell you of his death, Mr. Vaughan, for I have heard it from the lips of those that beheld it; and, more than that, I was the cause of it."

"How?" cried Vaughan, starting to his feet with sudden energy.

"Yes," repeated Hofer; "I was the cause of it. Do not shrink from me. Yet am I no murderer. My dying word I give you of this."

"Explain yourself," said Vaughan.

"I will. Sit down. Listen to me. The time may be short."

He paused and covered his face with his hands for several minutes, as if trying to bring the past thoroughly before his mind once

more. Then he raised his eyes again to those of Vaughan. They
were large, deep-set, and the Englishman felt the powerful and
picturesque form and face before him appeal loudly to his imagination as the sick man sat up suddenly with lighted eyes, and
spoke in a voice full of deep melody and impressive intensity of
tone: —

"It was in the year 1791, in the month of August, that I first saw
Mozart. I had only then lately returned from Spain, where I had
spent my youth. My family is, as you know, German. My uncle's
son, Hofer, married a sister of the composer; and he was one of
those who sang the 'Requiem' round the dying bed of Mozart.
Hofer had not the smallest idea of the manner in which I was concerned with the latter days of the great Wolfgang; and, indeed, I
think that I am bold and foolish in telling you of it now. However,
I know that your curiosity is excited, and you shall hear it. You are
aware that Salieri, the man whose long-tried hatred of Mozart
made him the object of suspicion after the death of the master,
thought fit to proclaim his innocence before several witnesses on
his death-bed at Venice, not many years ago. He was justified in
doing this: he had nothing to do with his death.

"When I arrived from Madrid there was a man of the name of
Schickaneder, the well-known manager of one of the theatres in
Vienna. He employed me as a copyist on one or two occasions and
I thus became acquainted with one of the greatest rascals in the
ranks of German managers. He was always in debt, tumbling into
it as fast as his friends helped him out. Yet was this rogue the
favorite of all who knew him, even long after he was detected in
tricks which might have sent him to gaol and a guillotine. He was
so mightily agreeable, so frank and joyous a companion, so irre-
sistibly droll and gay, that none could look grave in the festive
sunshine of his presence.

"This man had been for some time an acquaintance of Mozart
when I came to Vienna, and it was for him that the *Zauberflöte* was
composed — a work given to him under promise that he was not
to give it to the theatres of the city or country; a promise which he
broke in the most disgraceful manner, though he knew that his
want of honesty was severely felt by Mozart, who was in almost as
great need of money as he was himself. I have often wondered by
what law of nature it is that genius must be poor and improvident.
The sensitive temperament seems to require the scourge of want

to spur it on over the obstacles in its road; at least thus alone can I explain to myself the penury of the brilliantly gifted.

"Mozart was preyed upon by the neediest wretches in the city. Stadler and Artaria sucked his brains with as much ease of conscience as I would perform that office to an egg, and with the splendid prodigality of the heart of true genius, he forgave them their debts and mean offences. I must say, though, that when I first became acquainted with Schickaneder, and others of this class, I knew nothing of this, and supposed *him* at least to be as honest as most of the men we meet in the way of business.

"It was in May that Schickaneder was walking one day in the Prater with Mozart when I passed them. I looked with some curiosity on the latter, for I had never before had so good a view of him, however well I knew him from reputation. I saw the large, languid, and prominent eyes fixed on the face of the man to whom he was listening with intense earnestness. Schickaneder at that moment was describing to him the plan of the opera that he desired to have, and in which he proposed to sing himself. He looked on it as the means of extricating himself from difficulties and distress, and to this work Mozart was willing to lend a kind and helping hand. I turned round to look at them after they had passed, and compared with a smile the profiles of the two companions. Mozart's mountainous nose almost touched the tip of the chin of his friend, the latter being several inches taller than little Wolfgang. Mozart held him by the wrist, and they disappeared thus engaged in conversation round one of the wooded walks of the Prater.

"One evening in the month of August — early in the month; I think about the 7th or 8th, as far as I can recollect — I received a visit from Schickaneder and Stadler. They sat smoking and talking in my rooms for some time, and their conversation was entirely on the subject of the new opera, its probable success, and the means whereby they might conceal from the composer the treachery of which they had been guilty; for doubtless, you know that Mozart had generously given the *Zauberflöte* to Schickaneder for his benefit, under the promise that no copies were to be privately disposed of among the other theatres in the metropolis or in the country. This engagement had been broken through by Schickaneder; for he had furnished several managers with the score of the opera, and he had thus secured a handsome sum for himself.

"This conversation interested me, though I was not personally concerned in the transaction, and on that occasion Schickaneder entertained me and his companion with many anecdotes illustrative of the peculiar temper and taste of Mozart.

"Coarse fellow, and grotesque in the extreme as he was, he could enter into the minutest point of interest and peculiarity of character; and intimately acquainted as he was, too, with the private habits of the composer, he was able to give the most admirable sketches of his ways, his manners, his restless fits of wandering to and fro, his feverish fidgets when the brain was in labor of an air or an opera, and the most salient points were further illuminated by mimicry of the highest order; that power of imitation which nearly rises into inspiration, and appears capable of transfusing the very being, the thoughts, the powers almost, of another into the spirit of the actor for the brief instant of representation.

"Schickaneder had known 'old Leopold,' as he called him, the father of Mozart, for many years and he was especially happy in the performance of the scene supposed to take, or rather asserted to have taken place between father and son at a carnival ball, when Mozart, whose animal spirits at times rose above all control, enacted the part of Punchinello, and annoyed the more prudent parent by making in that character a deeper impression on society than old Leopold's circumspection deemed desirable.

"Do you know," said Hofer, after pausing for a few moments, "the struggles and distresses of genius are to me as a veritable vision of purgatory. Many, many were the clouds and billows that obstructed that spirit ere it took its white-winged flight to the stars, and enthroned itself in the everlasting serene of immortality."

Here Hofer paused, and remained silent for many minutes. At last he resumed his narrative, saying —

"You doubtless know the supernatural tradition of the stranger that visited Mozart, and who ordered him to write a requiem, to be ready by a certain day, and for which a certain sum was to be paid!"

Vaughan bowed in silence.

"Ah," replied Hofer, "who shall dare to raise the veil that shrouds the inner holy of holies of genius from the vulgarizing gaze and comments of lower and coarser natures? This I will tell you, however, that the wonderful organization of Mozart was one apt to tremble and vibrate beneath a breath, or swerve one tittle from its usual calm. I learnt that night from Schickaneder that two years before they had attended a masquerade together; that on that occasion he had seen the terrible superstition wherewith the poor, frail-hearted genius was cursed, and what had particularly recalled it to his mind was the fact that that very day Mozart had met him in the public walk, had drawn him aside, and had told him that the figure of the masqued fortune-teller who had prophesied his future fate to him at the masquerade two years before had appeared to him, and, lifting its disguise from its face, had shown him that of pale death, while the words 'Requiem aeternam' were breathed, more than spoken, by the unearthly messenger, sent, he believed, to warn him of his end. He appeared to be extremely nervous and depressed when he spoke of it, and added, that after starting up from his sleep, and walking to and fro in his room, he lay down again to rest, and that, while sleeping, a chorus of supernatural sweetness had sung to him a service for the dead — parts of which had escaped him, but parts of which he remembered still; and he had sung to Schickaneder a few bars of the tenderest and saddest melody. Schickaneder had laughed at him, not believing himself in anything of supernatural agency; but with wild and mournful earnestness Mozart had persisted in the truth of the visionary choir, and continued to repeat in a low tone, the words — 'Requiem aeternam dona eis, Domine.'

"The strong nerves and reckless, healthy spirit of the actor could not realize the morbid and miserable presentiment that hovered gloomily over the mind of the musician.

"Of that word, presentiment," said Hofer, looking steadfastly at Vaughan, "how little is comprehended by those who use it most glibly. The warning voice that fills the secret chambers of the imagination with a dread of coming woe and death, whence doth it arise? for what purpose? What spirit, good or evil, dare thus thrust its advising, its foreboding influence, between man and his fate? Rarely has a presentiment turned aside the blow that was to fall. The fated being feels — hears, as it were, the dread rustling of the wings of the coming Azrael; but he walks without stumbling to the encounter, and the warning voice has failed in its mission. Whence do these powers of prophecy arise, if we listen with our hands bound with the strong chains of fatality? I have known a man leave his home to take but a short excursion of pleasure, and with his eyelids as wet, ere he said farewell to his wife, as if he were bound for a field like the great Waterloo. He knew that he should return no more; but he *went*, and he was killed that afternoon in a pleasure-ground by accident.

"Well, I must tell you of the end of this adventure. Schickaneder and Stadler remained talking of the dark stories of dreams, witchcraft, and wonders of *diablerie*; and, on Stadler doubting the truth of the story told him by Schickaneder, of Mozart's superstitious dread excited by his late dream, Schickaneder protested that he would wager a considerable sum of money on the subject, and that he would half kill Mozart with fright by a trick, which would convince all Vienna of his foolish belief in supernatural agency."

"'There are,' he said, 'no bounds to the silliness of those who believe in the miraculous. I will engage to make Mozart believe that the evil one has come to him in person, and has made him promise him a requiem, to be ready by a certain day. Yes, I will wager you a hundred — two hundred francs — what you will.'

"'I accept it,' said Stadler, 'with all my heart, and I will fix the bet at two hundred and twenty francs.'

"'Done! said Schickaneder. 'You leave Vienna to-morrow, I know, and so you will not interfere with or disturb in any way, my arrangements. I will engage to furnish Vienna with a farce of my own at Mozart's expense.'

"They continued to talk for some time after this, and at last they left my house very late, having smoked and drunk for several hours in my upper room."

"It was on the following day, about five in the afternoon, that I saw Schickaneder again. He came, he said, to ask a favor of me; and on my saying that I would do anything in my power to serve him, (for the man was a favorite of mine,) he told me that he wished for my assistance in a trick that he was going to play to a friend. He described to me the part that he wished me to play. I was to be dressed in a suit of mourning with which he was to provide me. I was to go at nightfall to Mozart's dwelling, ask an audience, and enter his room with my hat slouching over my brows. I was not to remove it. I was to refuse to give my name. I was to offer any sum, and to name the day when it was to be finished. Schickaneder made me rehearse my part till I was perfect in it, and we performed it together, I acting the part of the mysterious visitant; he performing the terror-stricken artist to the life. I felt extremely amused, and longed to see the result of my *début*. It never occurred to me that real fear could be caused by so paltry a trick.

"It was on Thursday, the 11th of August, that I went to Mozart's house. It was about eight o'clock, and he was at supper with his wife. I said that I must see him, for my business was urgent; and as I stood waiting his approach, I myself became impressed with the idea — weak and foolish enough, too — that I *was* an appointed means of warning him of his coming end; and this, I feel sure, lent a solemnity and terror to my words and manner that they could not otherwise have possessed. I was left for some time alone, and I had time to examine the room of the genius. There was in one corner an open harpsichord, with a piece of manuscript music on the desk. A silk handkerchief, stained with ink, lay beside it, and a handful of flowers, faded with the heat, were tossed in a withered heap within the leaves of a copy of the *Zauberflöte.* He had been altering some of the concerted pieces to suit the fancy of Schickaneder, who made his appearance in the following month as Paragon, in the opera I have just mentioned. I stood immovable in the centre of the room, waiting anxiously for the appearance of my victim. Suddenly, without, I heard the voice of Schickaneder. He was in the house, and he accompanied Mozart to the door of the room in which I was. He stood at the entrance speaking cheerfully to the composer; and I retreated to the darkest corner of the room, almost wishing to make my escape unseen, when Mozart entered, and I saw in the pale twilight the faint outline of his head and form. He approached, and I rose and came forward. He spoke first in German. He said, —

"'I regret having kept you waiting, sir; what are your commands?'

"I replied in German. My speech was at that time slightly tinctured with a foreign accent, from having lived so long out of my native country. I suppose that this gave my voice and words a peculiarity that made them impressive. I have often thought that I might have succeeded as an actor; for I know not why, but I have observed through life that a chance word, or a look from me, has been held to contain much more meaning than I ever intended to give, and I imagine that this is owing to my appearance, manner, voice — my exterior in short, without any corresponding power in my internal being. It has led me into many strange positions, but I shall only mention this one for the present.

"My reply to Mozart was couched in the words agreed on between Schickaneder and myself. He had prepared me for the scene I had to perform; and I could not help marveling at the power of close imitation possessed by the actor, when I heard and saw the face, voice, and manners of our victim. He listened to my reply, which consisted only the words, —

"'I have come to request you to write a requiem;' and approaching me he said, in an uncertain voice, inclining his head forward as if anxious to inspect my face more closely —

"'May I ask for what personage of distinction?'

"Now Schickaneder had prepared me for this question, as one of the very first, probably, that would be put to me, and my reply had been dictated by him. I answered slowly —

"'You have said right: it *will be for a personage of distinction*, but I cannot reveal the name to you.'

"He was silent. Fear entered into him at that instant, the fear that dogged his steps; a hell-hound of superstition to the last instant of his life. He spoke at last in a husky and quivering voice, —

"'What are the terms you propose?'

"'Name them,' I replied. Mozart paused, and said, —

"'It is, then, for a prince?'

"'For *a person of distinction*,' I replied, very pointedly. He paused, and then turned quickly round on one heel, saying, —

"'How! a requiem for a living man?'

"I remained silent.

"'What say you to a requiem for a living man?' he repeated, rather impatiently.

"I replied as Schickaneder had told me to do, —

"'I can answer no questions; the requiem *must* be ready for a certain day, for it will be wanted.'

"'For a certain day!' said Mozart. 'What day?'

"'You shall name it,' I replied.

"He paused, staring at me, and then suddenly asked me to sit down, going to the door and calling on his wife, —

"'Stänerl! Stänerl! a light here!'

"He called twice, but his request was unattended to. She was out just then — the poor loving Constance! He came back, and again asked me to sit down; for I was standing in the same place, preparing to leave the room as soon as it was possible. I was obliged to keep up my character, you see, and I remained motionless, feeling that my presence, my words, were as terrible to my listener as those of a supernatural messenger. There was to me a certain degree of vivid pleasure in this position; and I imagine that the arch-rogue Cagliostro was very much of my way of thinking and feeling when he be-fooled Europe, and crowned quackery bowed down before him. I found that brevity made the deepest mystery in my case, and my great desire was to leave the room as soon as possible. I moved towards Mozart, who retreated from me as fast as I drew near him. At last he was pinned to the wall; his eyes were fixed on mine; I could hardly see the face or expression — nothing but the large nose, the most prominent feature of the kind that could be seen on any face in Vienna. I was near the door, and a table was placed to the right of where I stood. I laid down a purse containing twenty ducats, (Schickaneder had borrowed the greater part of this from a cousin, who assisted him sometimes in his necessities, and as I did so I said, —

"'Here are twenty ducats; you shall have as many more when *it is finished*. The time you must name.'

"'I will send it — I will send the requiem,' said Mozart, hurriedly; 'give me your address.'

"I merely shook my head, and remained silent.

"'Then to whom shall I transmit it?' he cried.

"'To myself,' I replied, quietly. 'I shall come to receive it when it is ready; name your day.'

"He was silent for several minutes; he seemed incapable of speaking.

"'I am engaged — very busily engaged,' he said, at last, with hesitation. 'I will endeavor to have it done — this autumn; why, this month, if you will.'

"I bowed in silence, but still waited for the day being specially mentioned. He seemed agonized with some very strong feeling of dread or anger. I wondered then, I wonder still, that he did not detect the charlatan before him, and dismiss me with a good beating; but my deportment was too imposing to permit an imaginative victim to escape its influence, and Mozart remained with his back glued to the wall, despair in his voice, and tears, I am almost sure, in his eyes, if I could have seen at all distinctly. He hesitated a good deal: at last he said —

"'I go to Prague in September; I am occupied in writing an opera for the coronation festival there. You see that I have a great deal on hand, but your offer shall be — must be accepted, I suppose. Yes, I accept it; and on the 3d of September you shall have it.'

"I bowed slowly and left the room, unaccompanied by Mozart, who remained standing, leaning against the wall, and let me depart without another word.

"I went to Schickaneder; he laughed heartily over my detailed account of the whole scene, and told me that I must go again on the 3d of September to claim the promised requiem. He was now anxious to make a good sum of money by it, for he prophesied that the result of this nervous agony would be the finest piece of sacred music yet produced by Mozart. He said that he would dispose of it in England, where he might hope to get a larger sum for it than anywhere else; and at such a distance his treachery was less likely to be found out. I promised to perform his bidding in September, and in the mean time he gave me a good deal of employment in copying out the orchestral and vocal parts of the new opera which was to be brought out the following month. I had no news of the requiem for three weeks nearly, but on the 3d I again went to Mozart's house, after assuming the same black dress I had worn on the first occasion. Schickaneder had come to my house on the evening of the 2d of September to tell me that Mozart, he had just heard, was to leave for Prague on the following day instead of the 5th, which had been his first intention — that, therefore, I must go by daylight next morning to claim the music, and that I must on no account let the opportunity slip, as he wished to have it in print as soon as possible. I went on the morning of the 3d to the composer's house; I requested an audience, and insisted on obtaining it. Three times he sent a woman-servant to know my name and my business: I refused to mention either. Mozart was at this moment on the point of departing for Prague. He was going with his wife and Süssmayer, his pupil; and I saw the two latter engaged in filling the vehicle in which they were to travel, and in which he wrote many of the best parts of the *Clemenza di Tito*. Composing to him was hardly a labor; his brain threw off music as naturally as fire does heat and light. That harmonious organization thought in melody and poetry as others do in unmusical prose. This was the secret of his marvellous industry, as people called it. It was not industry, but the facile prodigality of his nature venting itself in a thousand different channels — some sparkling with sunshine, others grave with shadows; and the brilliant torrent of his genius passed through all with an equal triumph, and it rings in our ears still with a lordly voice that time itself shall try in vain to silence.

"I stood, you must know, near the entrance, from which spot I could see the carriage, and I knew that he could not leave the house without passing me. At last he came, brushed past me, and sprung into the carriage. His wife was following him, but ran back to get something that she had forgotten. He called her impatiently twice, and I then came forward and stood before him. I put my hand on the door, and leaning forward I fixed my eyes steadily on those of Mozart. His face expressed the wildest terror; his cheeks were haggard and sunken; his eyes glared wide on me, and he seemed incapable of addressing me. I said to him —

"'Is the requiem finished?'

"'No! no!' he exclaimed, vehemently; 'I have not finished it, but I promise it in a month.'

"'I am satisfied,' I replied; and I drew back, lifting my forefinger slowly, and saying, 'On the 3d of October I shall come.'

"His wife entered the carriage; I did not stop to see their departure, but returned home, wondering at the power that I wielded over one so superior to other men in talent."

"And you went again?" said Vaughan, anxiously.

"No," said Hofer; "that was my last interview with the composer. When Mozart returned from Prague he found out the treachery of Schickaneder — not, however, till after the first performance of the *Zauberflöte*. It was then disclosed to the composer that the manager had disposed in secret a number of copies, and though Mozart's only exclamation was, 'The knave!' yet there was good reason to suppose that Mozart was about to call him to account, with the help of the law, for his dishonesty; and Schickaneder told me that he wished no more to be said or done in the matter in which I had been engaged.

"Now I will tell you of the last time that I saw Mozart: it was on the day that his 'Praise of Friendship' was performed at the Freemasons' meeting. It was received with a triumphant welcome, and I could distinctly see the face of Mozart. It was flushed with the gladness of a glorious success, and in that beaming face I could hardly have recognized the wan countenance I had looked on a few weeks before.

"This last glimpse I had of him was in the middle of November. From that day until the 21st of the same month he enjoyed the full sweets of his position as the greatest living composer. Numbers of orders for music of all kinds flowed in on him, and he stood smiling in the parting gleam of life's festal sunshine. But on the 21st he was taken ill: he had finished the 'Requiem' that day and the fact of no one coming to claim it persuaded him more firmly that it was for himself. He told this to my cousin Hofer, his brother-in-law, who tried to laugh him out of the belief of his approaching death; but the story got about in Vienna, and Schickaneder claimed his bet with Stadler, who returned to Vienna from Berlin on the following 1st of December. If I had been on good terms with Hofer I should have been much tempted to tell the truth to him, and thus relieve the dying man of his fears; but I did not feel disposed to do so, and I let things remain as they were. I will confess to you that my own impression in the years was that Schickaneder, knowing that his crop of golden eggs was at an end, disliked the idea of another profiting by his detection. Mozart had entered into an engagement to write three operas for Karl Behrisch, the manager of a rival theatre. Schickaneder knew that he was liable to heavy punishment for what he had done; he was drowned in debt, and the triumph of possessing Mozart's *last*-opera was too profitable a pleasure to be given up to another. Unless Mozart wrote another opera, nothing could eclipse the *Zauberflöte*; and he might hold all audiences captive with Mozart's last work, if Mozart died. If he lived, the scene would be changed. I believe that a diabolical prudence made Schickaneder poison him."

"How!" cried Vaughan.

"I cannot tell you *that*," replied Hofer; "but I will believe anything rather than that I frightened him to death."

170

APPENDIX

Sites around the world where the *Requiem* was performed on
September 11, 2002:

Country or Protectorate	State or Province	City	Time zone
New Zealand		Auckland	24
		Wellington	
Australia		Brisbane	22
		Sydney	
Japan		Nagoya	21
		Osaka	
		Tokyo	
Taiwan		Tapei	20
Thailand		Bankok	19
Russia		Samara	16
		Moscow	15
		Kaliningrad	14
Armenia		Yerevan	
Israel		Reut	13
		Tel Aviv	
Latvia		Riga	
Austria		Vienna	12
Belgium		Aalst	
Czech Republic		Pardubice	
Hungary		Kecskemet	
Lithuania		Vilnius	
Poland		Zabrze	
Spain		Almeria	
		Requetas de Mar	
Yugoslavia		Belgrade	
England	West Yorkshire	Bradley Near Keighley	11
Ireland		Cork	
Portugal		Lisbon	
		St. Domingos de Rana	
Suriname		Paramaribo	9
Puerto Rico		San Juan	8
Brazil		Manaus	
		Rio de Janeiro	
Canada	Newfoundland	Mount Pearl	
	Ontario	London	7
		Mississauga	
	Québec	Montreal	

	Manitoba	Flin Flon	6
		Winnipeg	
Haiti		Port-au-Prince	
Honduras		Tegucigalpa	5
United States	Alabama	Opelika	6
	Alaska	Homer	3
	Arizona	Phoenix	4
		Tucson	
	California	Aptos	3
		Berkeley	
		Bradbury	
		Burlingame	
		Marin	
		Monterey	
		Mountain View	
		Nevada City	
		Pasadena	
		Ranch Palos Verdes	
		Richmond	
		Rohnert Park	
		Sacramento	
		San Francisco	
		San Pedro	
		Santa Barbara	
		Santa Monica	
		Sonoma	
		Stockton	
		Valencia	
	Colorado	Boulder	5
		Fort Collins	
	Connecticut	Bloomfield	7
		New Canaan	
		Somers	
	Florida	Fort Pierce	
		Fort Myers	
		Jacksonville	
		Orlando	
		Tampa Bay	
		Winter Park	
	Hawaii	Honolulu	2
		Kauai	
	Idaho	Sandpoint	4
	Illinois	Arlington Heights	6
		Chicago	
		Lisle	

		Palos Heights	
	Indiana	Bloomington	
		Indianapolis	
	Iowa	Fairfield	
	Maine	Gorham	7
		Orono	
		Rockport	
		Topsham	
	Maryland	Annapolis	
		Baltimore	
		Salisbury	
	Massachusetts	Boston	
		Framingham	
		Newburyport	
		South Attleboro	
	Michigan	Ann Arbor	
		Grosse Pointe	
		Holland	
		Midland	
	Minnesota	Duluth	6
		Golden Valley	
	Missouri	Columbia	
		Saint Louis	
	Montana	Missoula	5
	Nebraska	Omaha	6
	Nevada	Elko	4
	New Hampshire	Kingston	7
		Nashua	
	New Jersey	Ridgewood	
		Summit	
		Woodbury	
	New Mexico	Santa Fe	5
	New York	Albany	7
		Batavia	
		Carmel	
		Huntington	
		Ithaca	
		Jamestown	
		Long Island	
		Lynbrook	
		Mount Tremper	
		New York	
		Potsdam	
		Poughkeepsie	
		Rochester	

		Scarsdale	
		White Plains	
		Woodstock	
	North Carolina	Charlotte	
		Lumberton	
		Pinch	
		Raleigh	
		Wilmington	
		Wingate	
	North Dakota	Bismark	6
	Ohio	Bowling Green	7
		Cleveland Heights	
		Cleveland	
		Columbus	
		Mansfield	
		West Carrollton	
	Oklahoma	Tulsa	6
	Oregon	Coos Bay/North Bend	4
		Portland	
	Pennsylvania	Allentown	7
		Carlisle	
		Harrisburg	
		Reading	
	Rhode Island	Riverside	
	South Carolina	Florence	
		York	
	South Dakota	Sioux Falls	6
	Tennessee	Memphis	
	Texas	Dallas	
		Houston	
		San Juan	
		Southlake	
	Utah	Salt Lake City	5
	Virginia	Charlottesville	7
		Fredericksburg	
		Hampden-Sydney	
		Harrisonburg	
		Southside	
	Washington	Aberdeen	
		Bainbridge Island	
		Longview	
		Olympia	
		Seattle	
		Snoqualmie	
		Spokane	

		Tacoma	
		Vashon Island	
		Wenatchee	
	West Virginia	Charleston	
		West Liberty	
		Parkersburg	
	Wisconsin	Madison	6
		Milwaukee	
Honduras		Tegucigalpa	5
American Samoa		Mapusaga	1
		Pago Pago	

Printed in the United States
25249LVS00001B/47

9 780875 863290